A DICTIONARY OF GUYANESE WORDS AND EXPRESSIONS

Daizal R. Samad

Ashwannie Harripersaud

BLUEROSE PUBLISHERS
India | U.K.

For permissions requests or inquiries regarding this publication, please contact:

BLUEROSE PUBLISHERS
www.BlueRoseONE.com
info@bluerosepublishers.com
+91 8882 898 898
+4407342408967

ISBN: 978-93-5819-087-8

Cover design: Tahira

First Edition: July 2023

PREFACE

Language as El Dorado's Gold

One Saturday, not long ago, one of the two contributors of this **Dictionary of Guyanese Words and Expressions** happened upon a Headmaster of a secondary school in Berbice. They met in the Port Mourant market. Both teachers, they chatted about goings on in their respective schools and about various matters educational, as teachers are wont to do. The contributor, Ashwannie Harripersaud, mentioned our work on this Dictionary. The headmaster asked: "Lemme ask you this, Miss. With all these people who say they teaching English, why did it take so long for anyone to do something like this?" Now that is a simple but interesting question. Why indeed?

The last noteworthy attempt at recording and explaining Guyanese words came from Harold Bascom. His **101 Words that tell you're Guyanese** was published in 2016. The remarkable work done on Guyana Creole by John Rickford, Dereck Bickerton, Richard Allsopp, Wordsworth MacAndrew, Walter Edwards and Ian Robertson must also be mentioned. It is worth noting, also, that four of these linguists/lexicographers were attached to the University of Guyana's Department of English in the 1970s and early 1980s.

Certainly, one of the most pivotal moments in the study of Guyanese words, came in 1975. It took the form of a public event we decided to call "**A Festival of Guyanese Words**". Most of the presenters were undergraduate students who were enrolled in a class taught by then Mr. John R. Rickford, a lecturer in the Department of English at UG. I was one of those under-graduates, and I remember having a discussion with John about the naming of the event: "conference" sounded stuffy and exclusive; "celebration" sounded a bit too trivial; so we settled on "Festival". It worked, and this event resulted in hundreds of attendees from the academic world, cane-cutters, hire-car drivers, teachers, businessfolk, civil servants, government officials, etc. The event also resulted in the publication entitled **A Festival of Guyanese Words**. The first edition of one thousand books were sold out in three days in Guyana. This led to a second edition.

This pivotal moment, wrought from the sweat of a great motivating, inspiring lecturer (now Distinguished Professor at Stanford University) and his second-year undergrads remains tragically unemulated. The question asked by the HM in Berbice returns: "With all these people who say they teaching English, why did it take so long for anyone to do something like this?" To be sure, university students in my day were no brighter than those of today. I can say that with certainty. It could be that we were more hungry than those of today. We read more, were more willing to take up challenges, were much less complacent, but no brighter. Could it be that the lecturers of today are less driven or that they are less inspiring? Maybe.

Or maybe those of us in academic circles who profess passionately our love for Guyana Creolese, those of us who would have Creolese as a National Language and medium of instruction, are so absorbed with the shallow politics of this stuff that the real work is abandoned. Maybe. Those of us in that circle hear the word "research" with sickening frequency, but nothing follows the babble.

Or maybe, more broadly, we as a nation are yet to learn about the vital role research plays in national development. Indeed, we seem to take little or no interest in our own history as Guyanese, as West Indians. When we come to the realization that our culture is inextricably entwined with our history, we may take an interest in both. And since language is welded to history and culture, we cannot study one without studying all. An article was published recently (by one of the two contributors to this Dictionary, interestingly enough) on the history of place names in Guyana. We may well ask: "Why was **this** not done before?"

This is precisely why the work by those scholars mentioned above remains outstanding, although with little visible follow-up from those that came after them. More specifically, Harold Bascom's **101 Words that tell you're Guyanese** (2016) stands alone. That is, until this **Dictionary of Guyanese Words and Expressions**. To be sure, because Guyana Creole is—like any active language—ever-evolving, the work will be ceaselessly unfinished. We can continue to hope that the next generation of Guyanese who are interested in our history, culture and language will be even more encompassing and penetrative than this **Dictionary of Guyanese Words and Expressions**.

There are differences between Bascom's work—the ancestor—and this Dictionary—the descendent. Bascom has the gift of humour and narrative; his story-telling talent shines through. **The Dictionary of Guyanese Words and Expressions** contains almost one thousand words and is more along the lines of the conventional dictionary; it is more comprehensive. It offers a guide to pronunciation via the International Phonetic Alphabet. It also offers examples of each word as it may be used in day-to-day conversation, and an approximate "translation" of those examples into formal English. Approximate because many of our Creole words have no English-language equivalent.

In the process of compiling this Dictionary, we were constantly reminded that there is no homogeneous Guyana Creolese. It is quite well known that "Town people" (Georgetown) speak quite differently from folks in Albion, say, in Corentyne Berbice. Even within Albion itself, the small village of Guava Bush has variations not used in Sand Reef, the former a stone's throw away from the latter. Guava Bush may be the only place on the planet where "bin" ends a sentence. Similarly, there are differences between the Creole spoken in Anna Regina and Charity, respectively, in Essequibo, as there are marked distinctions between the Creole spoken in Port Mourant to that spoken in Rose Hall Town, less than half of a mile away. We have tried through pronunciational and contextual examples of Creole lexical items to capture these differences. Readers may, for instance, notice some of our Creole sentences use "pickney" or "pickney dem" (to significant plurality) as against "chirrun" or "children". It is quite a valid question if one were to ask which Creolese we are talking about when we claim to be analysing or studying Guyana Creolese. This is one aspect of the complexity of Guyana Creole and therefore of any attempt to truly analyse, examine or record it.

The other complexity resides in the fact that each speaker's manner of speech (the register) will invariably change from circumstance to circumstance. The manner in which we speak at a parent-teachers' meeting is not the one we will use in our bottom houses talking to family members. Our Creole also shifts along the linguistic continuum depending on the topic of conversation. Our Creole shifts towards the basilectal (or deeper Creolese) end when we tell jumbie stories. It goes the other way when we speak nostalgically about our deceased parents or about school work. Moreover, we tend to shift when we are "gyaafin" with friends in the rum shop as against if we are speaking to a white person from America or Canada or England, say. The Creole also changes complexion from age-group to age-group. We may not be conscious of these shifts in register, but the shifts occur invariably.

All of this is to say that Guyanese Creole is something of a moving target to those who attempt to analyse it or make records of it. And, once again, Creolese grows with each new influence—especially with the injection of Americanisms: "like", "whatever", "should have", and "zupp", for instance. These may become a permanent feature of our Creole or simply be a passing fashion soon forgotten. Only the passage of time will determine if they become assimilated into the body of our Guyana Creole.

Unlike most of the Romance languages of Western Europe whose roots are grounded in Latin, Guyana Creole has many roots grounded in many languages (including Latin) from a multitude of places. Notice, for instance, that many of our schools have Latin mottos—the school I attended had the motto *"Per ardua ad astra"*, "Through hardships to the stars". Like our ancestry and our foods, our Guyana Creole is grounded in many soils. There are many languages from which we draw: the languages of our First Nations (or Amerindians); the many languages of Europe (English, French, Dutch, Spanish, Norse, Italian, Portuguese, etc.); the many languages of Sub-Saharan Africa (like the Gaa and Ashanti of Ghana, and from Yoruba and Ibo of Nigeria); the languages of China (Hakka, Hokkien, Mandarin, Cantonese, for instance); and the languages of North Africa and the Middle East. Because the British were our most prominent colonizers—affecting our behaviours, culture, dress, foods, and our language—the English Language offers up a kind of base upon which we place the other intersecting influences.   Our various religions too have their influences on our every-day language.

Guyana is El Dorado, city of gold. Of course, we mine literal gold in significant amounts. But our massive tropical rain forest to the south is also gold in terms of plant pathology and the medical benefits we are yet to mine. Our newly-found oil deposits are gold Our Atlantic to the north is gold for the wealth of marine life and potential for renewable energy. Our perennial summer is gold. Our Guyanese Creole is gold too, if we choose to mine it with scruple, with love.

Daizal R. Samad

Professor

University of Guyana

A a

abedeez /ɑbɪdiːz/

we, our

Example: *Abedeez poor, but abee naah stave.*

             We are poor, but we are not starving.

abee /ˈɑbiˈ/

two or more people referring to themselves

Example: *Abee ah guh fineral tomorrow.*

             We are going to a funeral tomorrow.

ajah /ˈɑːdʒɑˈ/

paternal grandfather

Example: *Ajah seh dat daady bin wan nice-nice baby.*

             Grandfather said that daddy was a beautiful baby.

ajee /ˈɑːdʒiː/

paternal grandmother

Example: *Ajee an ajah always fight bout wha fuh cook.*

             Grandmother and grandfather always argue about what to cook.

aks /ˈɑks/

to ask

Example: *He does always **aks** fuh wan small piece.*

He always **asks** for money.

all-in-waan /ˈɔːl-ˈɪn-wˈɑːn/

a dish primarily of rice with added vegetables, greens, meat or fish

Example: *Dem gaan seaside an cook wan big pat **all-in-wan**.*

They went to the seaside and cooked a big pot of **cook-up rice**.

aloo /ɑːlˈuː/

potato

Example: *The lil bai eat out all ah **aloo** curry.*

The little boy finished the **potato** curry.

am /ˈɑm/

third person pronoun

Example: *Me bin tell **am** fuh do he homework.*

I told **him** to do his homework.

anar /ˈɑnɑːr/

pomegranate

Example: *Dem get nuff-nuff **anar** tree in dem yaad.*

They have many **pomegranate** trees in their yard.

anti-man /ˈɑnti-mˈɑːn/

male homosexual; gay man

Example: *He does behave like wan real **anti-man** sometimes.*

     Sometimes he behaves like a **homosexual**.

apple-banana /ˈɑpəl-bɑnˈɑːnə/

a short type of banana whose flesh is denser

Example: ***Apple-banana** mo sweet dan lang banana.*

     Apple-bananas are sweeter than long bananas.

artee /ˈɑːrtʼiː/

to beg someone to do or give something

Example: *She mooma complain dat she gat fuh **artee** she data fuh eat.*

     Her mother complained that she must **beg** her daughter to eat.

awee /ˈɑwiː/

third person plural

Example: *Wen **awee** done wuk, **awee** does eat an sleep.*

     When **we** are finished working, **we** eat and sleep.

ayuh /ɑjˈʌ/

a group of two or more people exclusive of oneself

Example: *Ayuh done **ayuh** homewuk?*

                     Are **you** finished doing **your** homework?

B b

baaji /bˈɑːdʒi/

spinach or callaloo

Example: *She seh de dactah seh dat **baaji** good fuh she.*

She said the doctor told her that **spinach** was good for her.

baaji /bˈɑːdʒi/

clubs suit in a deck of cards

Example: *Me haan full wid hearts, an he haan full ah **baaji**.*

My hand had lots of hearts, and his hand had lots of **clubs**.

baba /bˈɑːbɑ/

affectionate term for a baby or lover

Example: *Dah ol man nice-nice; he does call everybady he **baba**.*

That old man is very nice; he calls everyone his **babies**.

babylon /bˈɑbɪlən/

police

Example: *Dem hire-kyaar man like complain bout **babylon**.*

Taxi drivers like to complain about the **police**.

badam-latcha /bˈɑːdɑm-lˈɑːtʃə/

a confectionary made mainly of sugar and flour

Example: *As soon as me put de **badam-latcha** pon me tongue, e melt.*

As soon as I put the **sweet** on my tongue, it dissolved.

badarashan /bˈɑdɑrˌæʃən/

troublesome

Example: *Dem pickney prapah **badarashan**.*

Those children are troublesome.

bad-eye /bˈæd-aɪ/

the evil eye that brings misfortune or illness upon someone

Example: *Me does always put wan tickah pon me pickney forehead to stave aaf **bad-eye**.*

I always put a dot of my infant's forehead to avoid him from getting the evil eye.

badman /bˈɑdmɑːn/

an aggressive person

Example: *E think he is wan **badman**, but wen e see police he run under e bed an hide.*

He thinks he is **aggressive**, but when he saw the police, he hid under his bed.

bagass /bɑgɑs/

the remnant of crushed sugarcane

Example: *Me daady does bring home **bagass** fuh light abee fireside.*

My father brings home the **remnants of crushed sugarcane** to light our fireside.

baigan /bˈeɪgən/

eggplant

Example: *Abee had fry **baigan** an roti dis maanin.*

We had fried **eggplant** and flatbread this morning.

bakoo /bˈɑkuː/

a short male human-like supernatural being

Example: *Dem people rich becaas dem does feed dem **bakoo** milk an banana.*

Those people are rich because they feed their **bakoo** milk and bananas.

balata /bɑlɑtɑ/

a tree resembling a rubber tree

Example: *Dem ol time people use to bleed **balata** tree fih mek ball fih play cricket.*

The old-timers bled the **balata** tree to make cricket balls.

ballafaiya /bˈɑlɑfˌeɪjə/

a very hot type of pepper

Example: *Me like put **ballafaiya** fuh mek me all-in-wan hat-hat.*

I like to put hot **pepper** in my cook-up rice to make it very spicy

balloon /bɑluːn/

condom

Example: *Dem bai fin wan set **balloon** unda Pearlie winda.*

The boys found many **condoms** under Pearlie's window.

bam-bam /bˈɑm-bˈɑm/

a warning that punishment is due

Example: ***Bam-bam** guh come becaas he get way from school.*

Punishment is due because he ran away from school.

bam-bam /bˈɑm-bˈɑm/

buttocks (usually of a child)

Example: *De baby get wan bad rash pon she lil **bam-bam**.*

The baby has a severe rash on her little **bottom**.

bamzee /bˈɑmziː/

buttocks

Example: De pickney try run before he kyan waak, an fall down pon he **bamzee**.

The child tried to run before he can walk and fell on his **buttocks**.

bandarah /bˈɑndɑrɑ/

a space in which food is stored for safety before a Hindu religious function

Example: Pandit bless ah food in de **bandarah** before abee coulda eat.

The pandit blessed the food in the **room** before we could eat it.

bando /bˈɑndoː/

a semi-circular accessory to keep a female's hair in place

Example: Ah lil gyaal wear wan nice **bando** pon she hair.

The little girl wore a pretty **band** on her hair.

banga /bˈɑʃgɑ/

hard round seed of orange-colored fruit used as marbles

Example: De boys eat nuff-nuff wara then use de **banga** fuh play enter-hole.

The boys ate many awara fruit then used the **seeds** to play marbles.

bangamaree /bˈaŋgamˌæɹiː/

a type of scaled fish

Example: *She husban like fry* **bangamaree** *mo dan curry* **bangamaree**.

Her husband prefers fried rather than curried **bangamaree**.

banga-season /bˈaŋga-sˈiːzən/

hard times

Example: *Aftah Chrismas season, abee does face* **banga-season**.

After Christmas season, we face **hard times**.

ban-karailee /bˈan-kˈaɹaɪli/

small bitter gourd

Example: **Ban-karailee** *hardly does deh maakit*.

Small **bitter gourds** are hardly found in the market.

bannah /bˈana/

term referring to a male

Example: *Dah* **bannah** *aalways in trouble!*

That **fellow** is always in trouble!

barah /bˈara/

a deep-fried dish of mainly flour and split peas.

Example: *Me like eat* **barah** *wid mango sour*.

I like to eat **barah** with mango sour.

barakat /bˈɑrɑkˌɑt/

good luck

Example: *Dis money likka e gat barakat; e nah done.*

This money seems to have **good luck**; it refuses to get spent out.

bare-back /ber-bɑk/

without condom

Example: *Dah mout-man boas dat e ride ah gyaal bare-back.*

That mouthy fellow boasted that he had intercourse with the girl **without wearing a condom.**

bare-yuh-shayfe /bˈer-jˈʌ-ʃeɪf/

carry one's burden; persevere

Example: *Times bin haad-haad, but me daady tell me fuh bare-me-shayfe.*

Times were very hard, but my father told me to **persevere.**

bartan /bˈɑrtɑn/

kitchen utensils

Example: *E wife gat fa wash nuff -nuff bartan wen she done cook.*

His wife has to do lots of **pots and pans** when she is finished cooking.

basa-basa /bˈɑːsə-bˈɑːsə/

to refuse an offer before eventually accepting

Example: *She does always mek **basa-basa** before me get she fuh eat.*

She always makes a **fuss** before I eventually get her to eat.

basha /bˈɑʃɑ/

a type of scaled fish

Example: *Steam **basha** is de bes way fuh cook am.*

The best way to cook **basha** is to steam it.

bat-ears /bˈɑt-eːz/

large jutting ears

Example: *Dem pickney laff Sarah becaas she get **bat-ears**.*

The children mocked Sarah because she had **large, jutting ears.**

batee /bˈɑti/

buttocks

Example: *De chile gat wan haad-bail pon he **batee**.*

The child has a boil on his **buttocks**.

bax /bˈɑks/

to hit with open fist

Example: *De bai daady drap a **bax** pon e rude son.*

The boy's father **slapped** his rude son.

bax book /bˈɑks bʌk/

to study, to read constantly

Example: *Dah gyaal nah like play; whole day, she a bax book.*

That girl does not like to play; she **studies** throughout the day.

bax-haan /bɑks-hɑːn/

informal communal savings pool

Example: *Nuff abee country people nah like go bank; abee does throw bax-haan.*

Many of us rural folks do not like going to banks; we prefer to save by throwing **box-hands**.

baylay /bˈeɪleɪ/

to roll out or flatten dough

Example: *Dem nowadays gyaal nah know fuh baylay roti.*

Young girls these days do not know to **roll out dough** to make roti.

baytah /bˈeɪtˈɑː/

son or younger male

Example: *Dah ol lady does treat she neighba son dem like she own baytah.*

That old lady treats her neighbor's sons as she does her own **son**.

baytee /bˈeɪtʼiː/

daughter or younger female

Example: *Dah ol lady does treat she neighba gyaal chirun like she own **baytee**.*

That old lady treats her neighbor's daughters as she does her own daughter

bazadee /bˈɑzɑdˌiː/

to become confused

Example: *E so **bazadee** e nah know e right haan from e lef haan.*

He is so **confused** that he does not know his right hand from left hand.

beat-man /biːt-mɑn/

a man who beats his wife, girlfriend, and/or children

Example: *Everybady know he ah wan bad **beat-man**.*

Everyone knows that he is **a man who beats his wife and kids**.

beeta /biːtɑ/

paddle-shaped wooden instrument used to wash clothes

Example: *De gyaal gaan seaside wid she bucket an **beeta** fuh wash clothes.*

The girl went to the seaside with her bucket and **beeta** to wash clothes.

beetee /bˈiːtˈiː/

buttocks

Example: *Lil Sammy slip an fall flat pon he **beetee**.*

Little Sammy slipped and fell on his **buttocks**.

belaway /bɫɑːwˈeɪ/

to waste

Example: *Me dat-in-law does prapah **belaway** meh son money.*

My daughter-in-law **wastes** my son's money.

belembee /bɛlˈɛmbiː/

a small green fruit sour to the taste

Example: *Abee does grin up **belembee** fuh mek peppa sauce.*

We grind **belembee** to make pepper-sauce.

belly /bˈɛli/

to have patience

Example: *She gat **belly** fuh deal wid nine pickney.*

She has **patience** to look after nine children.

belly-wuk /bˈɛli-wˈʌk/

diarrhea

Example: *Wen e drink nuff milk, e does get **belly-wuk**.*

She gets **diarrhea** when she drinks lots of milk.

belna /bˈɛlnɑ/

rolling pin

Example: *She use de same **belna** fuh bus e head dat she use fuh mek roti.*

She used the same **rolling pin** that she uses to cook roti to burst his head.

benab /bˈɛnæb/

a pointed, thatch-roofed structure of Amerindian origin

Example: *Dem call de big **benab** in Georgetown Umana Yana.*

The big **benab** in Georgetown is called the Umana Yana.

betruush /bɛtrˈuːʃ/

a tiny red insect

Example: *De lil chile roll pon de grass an **betruush** bite she up bad-bad.*

The little child rolled on the grass and **betes rouges** bit her severely.

bhais /bˈaɪs/

a very overweight female

Example: *He like laugh dem fat gyaal, an now he marrid wan **bhais**.*

He mocked fat girls and is now married to a **very fat one**.

big-eye /bˈɪg-ˈaɪ/

greedy; covetous

Example: *He so **big-eye** dat he tek three time mo food dan he kyan eat.*

He is so **greedy** that he took three times more food than he can eat.

big-foot /bˈɪg-fʊt/

elephantiasis

Example: *Nobady should laff **big-foot** people.*

No one should mock people with **elephantiasis**.

big-head hassar /bˈɪg-hɛd hˈɑsɑ:/

a type of heavily shelled fish

Example: *Some people prefer fuh eat **big-head hassar** more dan regular hassar.*

Some people prefer to eat **big-head hassar** over ordinary hassar.

big-jill /bˈɪg-dʒˈɪl/

a British Guyana penny

Example: *Me mooma still get ten **big-jill** from British times.*

My mother still has ten **pennies** from the British times.

big-mout /bˈɪg-mɑʊt/

tendency to speak out of turn or to speak loudly

Example: *He open e **big-mout** an let-out people business.*

He opens his **big mouth** and tells everyone's personal affairs.

bin /bˈɪn/

a past tense marker

Example: *Abee **bin** wedding house yesterday.*

We **went** to the wedding yesterday.

binna /bɪnɑ/

a past tense marker

Example: *Abee **binna** guh maakit wen da accident happen.*

We **were** going to the market when the accident occurred.

bini /bˈɪni/

young lady/woman

Example: *Dem young boys does whistle off dem **bini**.*

The young boys whistle at the attractive **young girls**.

birdee /bˈɜːdiː/

penis

Example: *He mooma always tell de lil bai fuh wash e **birdie** clean-clean.*

His mother always tells the little boy to wash his **penis** clean.

black-bush chicken /blɑk-bʌʃ-tʃɪkɪn/

eggplant

Example: *Dem Corentyne people does call egg-plant **black-bush chicken.***

Those Corentyne folk use the term black-bush chicken for **eggplant**.

blackout /blɑkaʊt/

interruption in the supply of electricity

Example: *We does pay good money fuh **blackout** instead ah power.*

We pay good money for **interruptions** instead of for electricity.

black-sage /blˈɑk-sˈeɪʒ/

a bush whose stalks may be used to clean teeth

Example: *Nuff people binna use **black-sage** fuh brush dem teet.*

Many people used the **black- sage [stalk]** to brush their teeth.

bladdah /blˈɑdə/

balloon

Example: *Dey full up de house wid **bladdah** fuh de baby birdday.*

They filled the house with **balloons** for the baby's birthday.

bladdah /blˈɑdə/

condom

Example: *Yuh know wha happen at dat party wen yuh see all dem **bladder** pon de floor.*

You can imagine what happened at that party when you see many used **condoms** on the floor.

blam /blˈɑm/

to slam shut

Example: *Wen she vex, she does **blam** all dem door haad-haad.*

When she is angry, she **slams** all the doors very loudly.

blank-bullet /blˈɑʤk-bˈʊlɪt/

a sterile male

Example: *Awee know that e does fire **blank-bullet** coz e kyaan breed e wife.*

We know that he is **sterile** because he cannot get his wife pregnant.

blow /blˈoː/

a person who is unfaithful to his/her spouse

Example: *Afta he wife gee e **blow**, he shame fuh show he face.*

After his wife was **unfaithful**, he was too ashamed to appear in public.

blue-sakee /blˈuː-sɑkiː/

a small, milk-blue bird

Example: *Every maanin dat **blue-sakee** does wake me up hitting e beak pon meh glass winda.*

Every morning that **bird** awakens me by hitting its beak upon my window pane.

bo-bo /bˈuː-bˈuː/

breast or nursing bottle

Example: *De gyaal laf-laf an complain dat she baby wake up three time a night fuh **bo-bo**.*

The girl complained smilingly that her baby awakens three times per night to be **breast-fed**.

boo-boo /bˈoʊ-bˈoʊ/

secretions from the eye; sleepy seeds

Example: *Every maanin wen meh wake up, meh eye full wid **boo-boo**.*

Every morning when I awaken, my eyes have **sleepy seeds**.

boosee /bˈuːsiː/

powdery dust from paddy shell

Example: *He wife does feed **boosee** to dem pig.*

His wife feeds **rice shells** to their pigs.

boots /bˈuːts/

generic name for all flat footwear

Example: *All dem school-gyaal an school-bai does wear **boots**.*

School girls and school boys wear **sneakers**.

bore /bˈoːr/

to pierce

Example: *Plimpla pon ah lime tree **bore** up Janny an draw blood.*

Thorns from the lime tree **pierced** Johnny's skin causing it to bleed.

bottom-house /batam-haʊs/

yard underneath the house

Example: *She always deh ah **battam-house** in she hammick.*

      She is always in her hammock **under the house**.

boujee /bˈaʊdʒiː/

brother's wife

Example: *She nah even know she brother wife name; she always call she **boujee**.*

      She does not know her sister-in-law's name; she calls her **boujee**.

boun-belly /bʌŋ-bɛli/

constipation

Example: *E eat so much banana dat he get **boun-belly**.*

      He ate so many bananas that he became **constipated**.

bowlin /bˈoʊlɪn/

a knot

Example: *He use wan **bowlin** fuh kyatch de wild haas in de field.*

      He used a **knotted rope** to catch the wild horse in the pasture.

bradam /brˈadam/

to fall or hit down with a thud

Exanple: *Ah baby fall **bradam** wen e try fuh waak.*

The baby **fell with a thud** when it tried to walk.

braigah /bɹˈeɪɡa/

to be proud of achievements

Example: *She get she two subjeck CXC an tun **braigah**,*

She got just two subjects at the CSEC and suddenly became **proud**.

braigah /bɹˈeɪɡa/

shameless

Example: *She does lie aal de time, an still **braigah**.*

She lies constantly but has **no shame** about it.

break /brˈeɪk/

to ejaculate

Example: *Dem gyaal does call he minute-man becaas he does **break** fas-fas.*

The girls call him minute-man because he **ejaculates** very quickly.

brick /brˈɪk/

any stone or pebble

Example: *Dem wutlis bai dem does pelt meh daag dem wid fine **brick**.*

Those naughty boys throw small **stones** at my dogs.

bringle /brˈɪŋgəl/

spotted animal, especially cow or dog

Example: *Dah lady get nuff-nuff **bringle** daag.*

That lady has many **brinded** dogs.

bringle /brˈɪŋgəl/

a type of unscaled fish

Example: ***Bringle** fish does taste nice wen yuh fry am.*

Bringle fish is tasty when fried.

bruk-mine /brˈʌk-mˈaɪn/

discourage

Example: *Wen yuh force pickney fuh study, dem kyan get **bruk-mine**.*

When you force children to study, they can become **discouraged**.

bruk-mout /brˈʌk-mˈaʊt/

mouthy

Example: *Dah lady kyaan keep secret; she get **bruk-mout**.*

That woman cannot keep a secret; she **talks too much**.

bruk-mout /brˈʌk-mˈaʊt/

a hard type of bun

Example: *Dem pickney nah able eat **bruk-mout** without milk.*

The children cannot eat that **hard bun** without milk.

bruk-neck /brˈʌk-nˈɛk/

a stretched tee-shirt or sock

Example: *E sacks get **bruk-neck** becaas e ah wear am every day.*

His socks are **stretched** because he wears them every day.

bruks /brˈʌks/

to be without money

Example: *Dah man rich, but he does dress like e **bruks**.*

That man is rich, but he dresses as if he was **penniless**.

bubee /bˈʌbiː/

breast

Example: *Dah gyaal nah get shame; e whole **bubee** ah show.*

That girl is shameless; her **breasts** are exposed.

buck /bˈʌk/

derogatory term for Amerindian

Example: *Abee does insult abee Amerindian people wen abee call dem **buck**.*

We insult our **Amerindians** when we refer to them as buck.

buckman /bˈʌkmɑn/

one shot of liquor

Example: *Dah man does drink wan **buckman** every maanin before he guh wuk.*

That man drinks a **shot of rum** every day before he goes to work.

budday /bˈʌdeɪ/

friend

Example: *Dah man does get vex-vex wen stranga call am **budday**.*

That man gets angry when strangers call him **friend**.

bukhta /bˈʌkhtɑ/

male underwear

Example: *Dem teef-man tek all he **bukhta** pon de cloze-line.*

The thieves stole all his **briefs** from the clothes-line.

bun-bun /bʊn-bʊn/

burnt food found at the bottom of the pot

Example: *Dem does gee dem daag all ah **bun-bun** from dem pat.*

They give the dogs all the **burnt** food from their pot.

bunbunai /bˈʌnbʌnˌaɪ/

quarrelsome

Example: *Dem does always complain how dem neighba like **bunbunai**.*

They always complain about their **quarrelsome** neighbors.

bunjay /bʌndʒeɪ/

a dry curry

Example: *Me data like **bunjay** duck curry mo dan wata-wata duck curry.*

My daughter prefers **dry duck curry** over duck curry with lots of gravy.

bun name /bʊn ne:m/

to gossip

Example: *Every time dem-dah meet-up, dem only ah*
bun name.

Every time they meet, they **gossip**.

buse /bju:z/

an agitated argument especially using foul words

Example: *Dah lady **buse** out she husban in front e*
frien dem.

That lady **cursed** her husband in the
presence of his friends.

bush /bˈʊʃ/

marijuana

Example: *Dem police arrest de man fuh sellin **bush***
to dem pickney.

The police arrested the man for selling
marijuana to children.

bushmaster /bˈʊʃmæstɚ/

a type of snake

Example: *De **bushmaster** wrap rung wan cow like de*
cow ah wan chicken.

The **snake** wrapped around the cow as if it
were a chicken.

bussin a lime /bʌsɪn ɑ lɑɪm/

hanging out with friends

Example: *Friday night me an meh fren dem bin*
                 bussin a lime.

                 Friday night my friends and I were
                 hanging out.

busy-busy /bˈɪzɪ-bˈɪzi/

a type of grass with long stalks

Example: *Sheer **busy-busy** ah grow in dah drainah.*

                 Lots of **reeds** are growing in that drain.

C c

cack-eye /kˈɑk-ˈaɪ/

lazy eye

Example: *He eye so **cack-eye** dat me nah know if e ah watch me or watch somebady else.*

His eyes were so **lazy** that I could not tell who he was looking at.

camoodee /kˈɑmuːdˌiː/

a large snake

Example: *De man seh dat de **camoodee** swallow he sheep whole just suh.*

The man complained that the **snake** swallowed his sheep whole.

casa-casa /kˈɑsɑ-kˈɑsɑ/

sour or rancid

Example: *Dah food bin in ah fridge so lang e tun **casa-casa**.*

That food was in the fridge for such a long time that it became **rancid**.

catchcatchai /kˈɑtʃkɑtʃaɪ/

quarrelsome

Example: *He seh dat he wife spen whole day a **catchcathai**.*

He complained that his wife spends the whole day **nagging.**

catcha /kɑtʃə/

a form of hide-and-seek

Example: *Dem pickney ah spen whole day just playin* **catcha**.

     Those children spend the whole day playing **hide-and-seek**.

catchar /k ɑtʃɑːr/

one who interferes to "spoil the fun"

Example: *Dah* **catchar** *mess up we party.*

     That **spoil-sport** messed up our party.

caxson /kɑːksəṇ/

lesbian

Example: *De lady seh dat she neighba data ah wan* **caxson**.

     The woman said that her neighbor's daughter is a **lesbian**.

chaathay /tʃˈɑːte/

to use the tongue to clean a plate or fingers after eating

Example: *She enjay ah food so much dat she eat am out an* **chaatay** *ah plate clean- clean.*

     She enjoyed the food so much that she ate it all and **cleaned the plate with her tongue**.

chachi /tʃɑːtʃi/

paternal uncle's wife

Example: *She busy ah cook fuh she **chachi**.*

She is busy cooking for her **father's brother's wife.**

chack /tʃak/

to keep from moving

Example: *Dem does use wood black fuh **chack** truck an kyaar pan Torani.*

On the ferry, *Torani*, they used wooden blocks to keep vehicles from **moving.**

chadar /tʃadɑːr/

bed spread

Example: *Me bin done tell ah gyaal fuh rub dem nasty **chadar**.*

I already told the girl to wash the dirty **bed spread.**

chahur /tʃˤɑʌr/

uncooked rice

Example: *Dem seh dat pregnant lady always like eat **chahur**.*

They say that pregnant women like to eat **uncooked rice.**

chamar /tʃamɑr/

person of lower caste

Example:
Ado dah man rich-rich, he does get an like wan real **chamar.**

Although that man is very rich, he behaves like a **lower caste person**.

chamkay /tʃˈamke/

to sway hips seductively

Example:
Ah gyaal does always pass by hey wid she **chamkay** waak.

The girl always passes by here with her **hip-swaying** walk.

chanay /tʃɑ:ne/

food that are deep fried

Example:
Dah man does help **chanay** puree at nuff-nuff weddin house.

That man helps to **fry** food at many weddings.

chanchee /tʃˈantʃi:/

the remnants from squeezing coconuts for oil

Example:
Dem pickney like **chanchee** wid sugar wen dem mooma mek cocnut ail.

The children like to eat the **squeezed remnants** with sugar after their mother makes coconut oil.

cheese /tʃˈiːz/

money

Example: *Dah youthman always beg he daady fuh gee he lil **cheese**.*

                        That youngster always begs his father for **money**.

cheezee /tʃˈiːzi/

vagina especially of a little girl

Example: *De lil gyaal granmooma warn she fuh wash she lil **cheezee**.*

                        The little girl's grandmother warns her to wash her little **vagina**.

chichiman /tʃˈɪʃɪmɑːn/

male homosexual

Example: *E fren dem seh he does talk name like wan real **chichiman**.*

                        His friends say that he gossips like a **homosexual**.

chicken-foot /tʃˈɪkɪn-fˈʊt/

a deep-fried, stick-like snack made mainly of split peas and flour

Example: *Me does use nuff dhal fuh mek **chicken-foot**.*

                        I use lots of split peas to make **chicken-foot**.

chicknah /tʃˈɪknɑ/

side-dish

Example: *Me mooma cook dhal an rice an she fry
fish fah chicknah.*

My mother cooked dhal and rice, and she
fried fish as a **side-dish**.

chico /tʃˈɪːkoː/

generic name for all chewing gum

Example: *De gyaal seh she daady bring back nuff-
nuff chico from Merica.*

The girl said that her father brought back
lots of **chewing gum** from America.

chinee /tʃɑɪniː/

Chinese

Example: *Dese days dem get nuff chinee shap in
Corentyne.*

Nowadays we have many **Chinese** shops in
Corentyne.

chinky /tʃɪŋkiː/

Chinese

Example: *Me pickney get lil-lil chinky eye.*

My child has very small **Chinese** eyes.

chokha /tʃˈoːkɑ/

any food which has been steamed, boiled, or roasted and then mashed

Example: *Fish **chokha** does wuk good wid dhal an rice.*

Boiled and mashed fish goes well with split peas and rice.

chotoo /tʃˈoːtu/

small in size

Example: *Ray look **chotoo** near e buddy dem.*

Ray was **small in size** compared to his brothers.

chowkee /tʃˈaʊki/

roti board

Example: *Dah man in Port Mourant binna mek **chowkee** an belna.*

That man in Port Mourant made **rolling boards** and rolling pins.

chuk /tʃˈʌk/

to squeeze someone's throat with aggression

Example: *Dem police **chuk** up de beatman an trow e tail in jail.*

The police **choked** the violent man and put him in prison.

chungkaay /tʃˈʌɟkaːi/

when spices are added to hot oil

Example: *Me aantee **chungkaay** ah dhal wid nuff-nuff jeerah an gyarlic.*

My aunt **sautéed** lots of cumin and garlic and added that to the dhal.

churile /tʃˈʌːraɪl/

a supernatural being; the spirit of a woman who died in child-birth

Example: *Dem schupit people put ah baby in de same room as wan **churile**.*

Those stupid people put the baby in the same room as the **woman who died in child-birth.**

churkee /tʃˈʌrki/

a small patch or clump of hair left after the head is shaved

Example: *Abee pandit get wan **churkee** pan e head since e daady dead.*

Our pundit has a **small tuft of hair** after his head was shaved for his father's passing.

churus /tʃʌrʌs/

cigarette

Example: *Dah bai does always beg fuh wan **churus** plus wan light tuh.*

That boy always asks for a **cigarette** and a light besides.

clap /klɑp/

to pat gently

Example: *If she nah **clap** ah baby, e nah does doh-doh.*

If she does not **pat** the baby, it does not sleep.

cochar /ko:tʃɑ:r/

one who persuades someone else to do something to their benefit, to bribe

Example: *Da scamp-man try **cochar** me fuh help e teef ah man bicycle.*

The scoundrel tried to **persuade** me to help him steal the man's bicycle.

cochor /k'o:tʃo:r/

to flatter

Example: *Dah bai full ah **cochor** wen he wan use people.*

That boy **flatters** people when he wants to use them.

cochor /k'o:tʃo:r/

to gossip

Example: *Meh neighba dem gat nuttin fuh do but **cochor** bout dis an da bady.*

My neighbors do nothing else but **gossip** about everyone.

cocobeh /kʌkʌbɛ/

leprosy

Example: *Dem does scaan ah bai just becaas e get*
              cocobeh.

              They scorn the boy because he has **leprosy.**

colgate /kˈɑːlgeɪt/

generic name for all toothpaste

Example: *A dactah seh Crest **colgate** good fuh meh*
              teet.

              The doctor told me that Crest **toothpaste** is
              good for my teeth.

coocoobellee /kˈuːkuːbˌɛliː/

a small fish

Example: *Wen we pick up we drinks, we does aada*
              *fry **coocoobellee** becaas yuh can just chew*
              an swallow.

              When we are drinking, we order fried
              coocoobellee because they are easy to eat.

cool girl /kuːl gjʌrl/

cold beer

Example: *De place so hat dat we march to de beer*
              *gyarden and order two **cool girls**.*

              The place was so hot that we went to the
              beer shop and ordered two **cold beers**.

coolie /kˈuːli/

derogatory term for East Indians

Example: *Plenty people tink dat all dem **coolie** man does drink up dem rum an beat up dem wife.*

Lots of people believe that **East Indian** men always drink rum and beat up their wives.

cow-itch /kˈaʊ-ˈɪtʃ/

an itchy bush rubbed on the genitals of horses believed to make them run faster

Example: *Me see dem rub **cow-itch** pan ah haas wid meh own two eye.*

I saw them rub the **cow-itch leaf** on the horse.

craas /krˈɑːs/

unlucky, cursed

Example: *De man seh he so **craas** he kyaan win nuttin.*

The man said that he was so **unlucky** that he could not win at anything.

crabdawg /krˈɑbdɑːg/

person who cheats and lies

Example: *Afta me help dah **crabdawg** he come an teef pon me.*

Even though I helped that **animal**, he came into my home and stole.

crappo /krˈɑpoː/

frog

Example: *Some people does call **crappo** mountain chicken.*

Some people call **frogs** mountain chicken.

cratchetee /krˈɑtʃɪtˌiː/

grumpy

Example: *Nobady know why dah ol man always **cratchetee**.*

No one knows why that old man is always **grumpy**.

cruttah /krˈʌtˈɑː/

to nag or quarrel

Example: *Dah lady does fine any excuse fuh **cruttah**.*

That woman **quarrels** for any reason.

cungsi /kʊŋsi/

feces; to defecate

Example: *Ah stray cat **cungsi** pon meh bridge.*

The strayed cat **defecated** on my bridge.

curaas /kʌˈrɑːs/

a type of unscaled fish

Example: *Plenty people mout does swell up wen dem eat **curaas**.*

Many people are allergic to the **curaas** fish.

curry /k'ʌːri/

generic name for every side dish served with a meal

Example: *She husban beg she fuh cook ockro **curry** an rice.*

        Her husband begged her to prepare **fried** okra and rice.

cut-eye /k'ʌt-'aɪ/

to communicate displeasure or disapproval

Example: *De gyaal dash waan **cut-eye** pon de bai wen e get fresh wid she.*

        The girl gave him a **sharp disapproving look** when he became too forward.

cutlish /kʌtlɪʃ/

cutlass

Example: *Dem cane-cutta get som shaap-shaap **cutlish** fuh cut cane.*

        Those cane harvesters have very sharp **cutlasses** with which they cut sugar cane.

cutters /k'ʌtɚz/

finger-food

Example: *Nuff man in Guyana gat fuh get **cutters** wen dem drink.*

        Many Guyanese men must have **finger-foods** when they drink.

cyanta /kyæntɑ/

generic name for all four-wheeled trucks

Example:	*Jason does drive wan Leyland **cyanta** fuh fetch san.*
	Jason drives a Leyland **truck** to carry sand.

cyar-man /kyˈaːrmɑn/

car driver

Example:	*Hire-**cyar man** does always complain bout police.*
	Hire-**car drivers** always whine about traffic police.

D d

daab /d'ɑ:b/

to spread thinly

Example: *Me maamy use to mix mud an cow-dung fuh **daab** she battam house smood-smood*

My mother used to mix mud and cow feces **to spread** over the bottom of her house until it was very smooth.

daayin /d'ɑ:jɪn/

someone who nags perpetually

Example: *She husband seh she wan real **daayin**.*

Her husband said that she is **a perpetual nag**.

dabbit /d'ɑbɪt/

sister's husband

Example: *Me sista does always complain bout how much meh **dabbit** does drink.*

My sister constantly complains about **my brother-in-law's** drinking.

dada /d'ɑ:dɑ/

eldest brother

Example: *Wen me daady dead, meh **dada** bin tek care of all awee.*

After my father died, my **eldest brother** took care of all of us.

dah /dˈɑː/

that

Example: *Dah ting he duh not a good ting fuh duh.*

That thing that he did is not a good thing to do.

dah-side-ova /dɑ-sɑɪd-oːvɑ/

on the opposite side

Example: *Ah chuch deh dah-side-ova ah trench.*

The church is on **the other side** of the stream.

dakolay /dˈɑkolˌe/

to gulp down a liquid

Example: *He naah drink rum; he does dakolay am.*

He does not drink rum; he **gobbles** it.

dali /dɑːli/

doll

Example: *Wen me bin wan lil gyal, me daady bin buy nuff-nuff dali fuh meh.*

When I was a little girl, my father bought many **dolls** for me.

damkaray /dˈɑmkɑrˌeɪ/

to cure illness by blowing and chanting

Example: *Dem call in wan majee fuh damkaray ah pickney.*

They called in a religious leader **to cure** the sick child.

dan-dan /dˈɑn-dˈɑn/

clothes

Example: *Me dress meh pickney in nice-nice **dan-dan** fuh go ah Christmas party.*

I dressed my child in nice **clothes** to go to the Christmas party.

dandra /dˈɑndrə/

money

Example: *Back in de day, abee does call money **dandra.***

In the old days, we called **money** dandra.

dash /dˈɑʃ/

to hit or throw

Example: *Dah bai **dash** waan set mud pon meh pickney.*

That boy **threw** lots of mud on my child.

datchnah /dˈɑtʃnɑ/

money

Example: *Meh mooma does hide she **datchnah** in wan tailee.*

My mother hides her **money** in a cloth pouch.

dead-house /dɛd-haʊs/

home of a recently deceased person

Example: *Some people does guh **dead-house** jus fuh play domino.*

Some people go to **a wake** simply to play dominos.

deeds /diːdz/

dues; debt

Example: *Afta she laas de bet, she had fuh pay she **deeds**.*

After she lost the bet, she had to pay her **debts**.

deh /dɛ/

there

Example: *Me ah guh **deh** fuh buy wan bread come back.*

I'm going **there** to buy a bread and return.

deh /dɛ/

to be okay

Example: *Aunty Betty aks me how me **deh.***

Aunty Betty asked me if I am **okay**.

deh /dɛ/

in that particular place

Example: *Ah book **deh** pan ah table.*

The book is **on** the table.

deh /dɛ/

to be intimate

Example: *Meh hear seh dat dem two bin **deh**.*

I heard that those two were **lovers**.

deh /dɛ/

greeting

Example: *De teacha aks how abee **deh**, an abee ansa dat abee **deh**.*

The teacher asked **how we were doing**, and we answered that we were **okay**.

deh /dɛ/

after an interrogative

Example: *How me guh know wah dem ah duh **deh**?*

How would I know what they are doing **there**?

dem-seh-she-seh /dɛm-sɛ-ʃiːsɛ/

gossip

Example: *Dat lady always wid she **dem-seh-she-seh**.*

That woman is always **gossiping.**

desuh /dɛsʊ/

to be there

Example: *Meh ah guh **desuh** come back.*

I'm going **there** and coming back.

didi /dˈidi/

eldest sister

Example: *Me **didi** use to look afta meh likka me bin
she own-own pickney.*

My **eldest sister** cared for me as if I were
her very own child.

dig-she-out /dɪg-ʃi-aʊt/

to have had intercourse with

Example: *Ramchan boas dat he done **dig-she-out**, but
abee know e lie.*

Ramchand boasted that he already had
intercourse with the girl, but we knew he
was lying.

dis-side-ova /dɪs-saɪd-oːvɑ/

on this side

Example: *Ah chutch deh **dis-side-ova** ah road.*

The church is **on this side** of the road.

doh-doh /dˈo-dˈo/

sleep

Example: *She does put ah baby fuh **doh-doh** before
she cook dinna.*

She puts the baby to **sleep** before she
prepares dinner,

dohsay /dˈoseɪ/

pancake

Example: *She husban seh he wan **dohsay** an fry egg fuh tea.*

Her husband wanted **pancakes** and fried eggs for breakfast.

don'-feel-no-way /don-fil-no-weɪ/

do not feel badly

Example: *Meh done tell e **don-feel-no-way** dat me nah bin guh e daady funeral.*

I already asked him not to **feel badly** that I did not attend his father's funeral.

double-bank /dˈʌbəl-bˈaɟk/

joint effort

Example: *De overseer tell we dat if we **double-bank** de wuk, we gon done in half de time.*

The overseer told us that if we **work together**, we will finish off the work in half the time.

douglah /dˈʌglɑ/

mixed race

Example: *We bin always tink dat **douglah** children mo smart an strong.*

We always thought that **mix-race** children were brighter and stronger.

drainah /dɹˈeɪnɑ/

water way; gutter

Example: *Dem people does clog up de **drainah** wid dem garbage.*

Those people always clog up the **drain** with their garbage.

drapsee /dɹˈɑpsiː/

sleepy

Example: *E does always just siddung an drap sleep like e get **drapsee**.*

He always sits and falls asleep as if he had a **sleeping illness**.

drinks /dɹˈɪŋks/

generic name for all soda

Example: *Dem does gee dem pickney too much blak **drinks**, so e get fat-fat.*

Their child is over-weight because they give him too much **Pepsi**.

drungid /dɹʌŋgɪd/

to drown

Example: *Wen me bin wan lil bai, me bin almos **drungid** in Albian trench.*

When I was very young, I almost **drown** in the Albion trench.

duff /d'ʌf/

dumpling

Example: *Me nani does mek sup wid provision an* ***duff***.

My grandmother makes soup with provisions and **dumplings**.

duh-fuh-duh-nah-obeah /dʌ-fʌ-dʌ-na-objɑ/

it is not magic when we do favors for each other

Example: *Me do he wan favah, then wen e duh me wan favah, me tell am seh **duh-fuh-duh-na-obeah***.

I did him a favor, and when he did me a favor in return, I told him **dat it is not magic when we do favors for each other.**

duksee-duks /d'ʌksi:-d'ʌks/

aged juiceless coconut

Example: *Dem so bad, dem sell ah ol lady **duksee-duks** cocnut*.

They are so bad that they sold the old woman **extra dry** coconut.

dulaha /dʌl'ɑhɑ/

bridegroom

Example: *De **dulaha** tell de dulaheen fadda dat he want wan house before e eat.*

The **bridegroom** demanded a house from the bride's father before he ate the wedding food.

dulaheen /dˈʌlɑhɪn/

bride

Example:	*De **dulaheen** wear wan nice-nice red sari fuh marrid.*

The **bride** wore a very pretty sari in which to get married.

dular /dˈʌlɑɪ/

affectionate

Example: *Dah pickney prapah know fa show **dular** wen e wan something.*

That child knows well to show **affection** when he wants something.

dunda-head /dˈʌndə-hˈɛd/

stupid/foolish

Example: *Ah lady call e son wan **dunda-head** becaas e fail e tes.*

The woman called her son **stupid** because he failed his test.

dunkaydam /dˈʌʄkeɪdɑm/

do not care a damn

Example: *Too much Guyanese get wan **dunkaydam** attitude.*

Too many Guyanese have a **careless** attitude.

duro-duro /dˈʌrʌ-dˈʌrʌ/

a lot

Example: *Dah teecha gyaal get shoes **duro-duro**.*

That female teacher has **many** pairs of shoes.

dutchman /dˈʌtʃmɑːn/

supernatural being; spirit of a deceased male Dutch colonizer

Example: *Children kyaan play under dat tree becaas **dutchman** bury e money deh.*

Children cannot play under that tree because a **dutch spirit** buried his money under it.

dutee /dˈʌtˈi/

dirt

Example: *Ah bina scattah nuff-nuff **dutee** pan ah road.*

The rice harvester scattered lots of **dirt** on the road.

dutee /dˈʌtˈi/

nasty

Example: *Dah restaurant too **dutee** fuh me buy food deh.*

That restaurant is too **dirty,** so I do not buy food from there.

E e

ears ah ring /eːz ɑ rɪŋ/

ringing in the ears signifying that someone is talking about you

Example: *Wen me **ears ah ring**, me know dem binna taak bout meh.*

When my **ears started ringing**, I knew that they were talking about me.

ears-hole /eːz-hoːl/

passage leading to the eardrum

Example: *Dem teecha gat fuh punish da bai who juk meh son **ears-hole** wid wan pencil.*

The teachers should punish the boy who put a pencil in my son's **ears.**

e-batee-ah-bite */i-bati-a-baɪt/*

scared

Example: *Wen he does see meh daag, **e-batee-ah-bite**.*

When he sees my dog, he gets **scared**.

ee wuk /ˈiːwˈʌk/

tasty

Example: *De man stuff e mouth, shake e head, an seh: "Dis food **wuk**!"*

The man filled his mouth, nodded, and said: "This food is **good**."

e-gat-bad-mout /i-gɑt-bad-moʊt/

a person whose predictions about bad luck always come true

Example: *E bad-mout does crass people.*

       The **word from his mouth** always jinxes people.

eh-eh /ˈɛ-ˈɛ/

no

Example: *Me ask meh daady if me kyan come to yuh birdday party, but he seh **eh-eh**.*

       I asked my father if I can come to your birthday party, but he said **no.**

eh-heh /ˈɛ-hˈɛh/

yes

Example: *Meh kyan cum to yuh party if meh daady seh **eh-heh**.*

       I can come to your party if my father gives the **okay.**

e mout sweet /ˈi:-maʊt-swˈi:t/

someone who likes sweet or tasty foods

Example: *Dah pickney maamy does always taak bout how **e mout sweet**.*

       The child's mother always boasts about her son's **love of treats.**

e nah get wan pat fuh piss in /i nɑ gɑt wɑn pɑt fʊ pɪs ɪn/

impoverished but arrogant

Example: *E like big up e damn self, but **e nah ge wan pat fuh piss in.***

    He is arrogant and boastful, but he is **very poor**.

enta-hole /ˈɛntɑ-hˈol/

a children's game played with marbles

Example: *Ol people does gyaff bout how chirren dese days only know cell phone; dem nah play **enta-hole** an tagga no mo.*

    Old folks talk a lot about children being on cell phones, but do not play activity-based games, including **enter-hole**.

eye jump /ɑɪ-dʒʌmp/

twitch in the eye signaling bad luck

Example: *Wen meh **eye jump**, me does know something bad guh happen.*

    When my **eye twitches**, I know something bad will happen.

eye-nah-see- haat nah bun /ɑɪ-nɑ-si-hɑːt-nɑ-bʌn/

what cannot be seen cannot hurt you

Example: *Harry seh e nah bin know wah e son duh, so meh tell am seh **wah eye-nah-see-haat-nah-bun.***

    Harry did not know what his son did, so I told him what he **did not see cannot hurt him**.

eye-pass /ɑɪ-pɑːs/

a person who fails to show appropriate respect or
consideration

Example: *Dem does low dah bai fuh **eye-pass** dem
too much.*

They allow that boy to **disrespect** them.

eye-wata /ˈaɪ-wˈɑːtˈɑ/

tears

Example: *Dem lady binna laff-laff pan ah bus, but
wen dem land ah dead-house, sheer **eye-
wata** ah flow.*

Those women were laughing loudly on the
bus, but as soon as they landed at the
funeral, they shed lots of **tears**.

F f

faam-boad /fˈɑːm-bˈoːd/

form board

Example: *Abee buy nuff-nuff **faam-board** fuh mek kangreet drainah.*

We bought lots of **form board** to make a concrete drain.

fat-eye /fɑt-aɪ/

a glance at the private part of a woman

Example: *Only bad-hooman does gee nuff **fat-eye** fuh people see.*

Only prostitutes expose their **privates** to people.

fayah /fˈɑɪɑ/

fire

Example: *Wen yuh play wid **fayah**, yuh does get bun.*

When you play with **fire**, you get burned.

fayah-eye /fˈeɪɑ-ˈaɪ/

covetous person

Example: *Dah gyaal get **fayah-eye**: evryting she see she want.*

That girl is **covetous**: everything she sees, she wants.

fayah-rass /fˈeɪɑrɑːs/

super-natural being who sheds her skin and feeds on the blood of babies

Example: *Dem man fine ah **fayah-rass** skin an rub nuff-nuff peppa pan am.*

The men found the **fire-rass'** skin and rubbed lots of pepper on it.

fine-bud /fˈaɪn-bˈʌd/

a type of small edible bird

Example: *Uncle Samuel does always order **fine-bud** fuh eat wen he does pick up he drinks.*

Uncle Samuel always orders fried **bird** when he drinks.

fits /fɪts/

an epileptic fit

Example: *Dem teecha nah know wah fuh do wen de gyaal get **fits**.*

The teachers did not know what to do when the girl had an **epileptic fit**.

five-finga /fˈaɪv-fɪŋgɑ/

star fruit

Example: *Some people does call **five-finga** star fruit.*

Some people use the name star fruit for **five-finger**.

foo-foo /fˈuː-fˈuː/

a dish of pounded green plantains

Example: *We maamy cook **foo-foo** an fry-fish fuh dinnuh.*

Our mother cooked **foo-foo** and fried fish for supper.

foot /fˈʌt/

generic name for the entire leg

Example: *De dac seh meh pull wan hamstring in meh **foot**.*

The doctor said that I pulled a hamstring in my **leg**.

footsie-wootsie /fʌtsiː-wʌtsiː/

lovers or small children touching feet

Example: *We know dem deh wen we see dem playing **footsie-wootsie** under de table.*

We knew that they were lovers when we saw them **touching feet** under the table.

force-ripe /fˈoːs-rˈaɪp/

fruit or person that ripens or matures too quickly

Example: *Some maakit people does spray mango fuh **force-ripe** dem.*

Some market sellers spray mangoes to **quicken the ripening process**.

French-letter /frɛnʃ-lɛtə/

condom

Example:

*Meh almos faint wen wan **French-letter** fly out me aantee window.*

I almost fainted when I saw a **condom** fly out of my aunt's window.

fresh /frˈɛʃ/

shower

Example:

*De solja-bai seh he gat fuh grab a **fresh** before he guh back to wuk.*

The soldier said that he had to grab **a shower** before he goes back to work.

fresh /frˈɛʃ/

to flirt

Example:

*Me daady slap de drunk bai wen he try get **fresh** wid me.*

My father slapped the drunk boy when he tried to **flirt** with me.

G g

gains /gˈeɪnz/

to be fed-up of the same food or fruit

Example: *Meh eat chicken curry every day fuh two week till me gains am.*

I ate chicken curry every day for two weeks until I am **fed up** with it.

gata /gˈaːtˈɑ/

hard candy

Example: *Ah gata sweet but e so haad e cyan bruk meh teet.*

The **candy** was sweet, but it was so hard it could have broken my teeth.

get de itch /gɛ di itʃ/

irresistible urge to gamble

Example: *He get the itch, so e gaan an gamble.*

He had the **urge**, so he went to gamble.

goadie /gˈoːdi/

swollen testicles

Example: *Dem school bai tease de man bout he goadie.*

The schoolboys teased the man about his **swollen testicles**.

goatay /gˈoːtˈe/

to stir quickly, especially split peas

Example: *Me aantee **goatay** ah dhal good-good till e smood likka wata.*

My aunt **stirred** the dhal so well that it was as smooth as water.

goat-stone /gˈot-stˈoːn/

a sweet dish made mainly of flour and sugar

Example: *Me uncle does eat so much **goat-stone** dat he get diabetes.*

My uncle ate so much of the **sweet meat** that he got diabetes.

good-fuh-nuttin /gˈʌd-fˈɑ-nˈʌ tn̩/

worthless

Example: *He mooma spail da bai an e tun out to be waan **good-fuh-nuttin**.*

His mother so spoiled that boy and he turned out to be **worthless**.

goo-goo-man /guguː-mɑːn/

imaginary spirit used to scare children

Example: *Ah lady frighten ah pickney dat **goo-goo-man** guh ketch am if he nah eat e food.*

The woman scared the child that the **spirit** will get him if he does not eat his food.

greenheart /grin-hɑrt/

a type of popular hard wood

Example:	*Me glad meh mek me floor wid greenheart wood.*
	I was glad that I made my floor with **greenheart** wood.

grine name /gɹˈɑɪn neːm/

gossip

Example:	*Every time dem neighba meet up, dem ah grine mattee name.*
	Every time the neighbors get together, they **gossip** about each other.

guana /gwˈɑːnɑ/

iguana

Example:	*Wen yuh cook guana, yuh mus mek sure to tek out dem bittah gland.*
	When cooking *iguana*, be sure to remove the bitter glands.

guh /gˈʌ /

to go

Example:	*Dem ah guh maakit fuh buy fish.*
	They **are going** to the market to buy fish.

gulab-jamoon /gˈʌlɑb-dʒˈɑmuːn/

a sweet dish made mainly of powdered milk

Example: *Dem Haribole people prapah know fuh mek **gulab-jamoon**.*

Those Haribol people can make excellent **gulab-jamoon**.

gulgulah /gˈʌlgʌlɑ/

a sweet dish made mainly of bananas

Example: *Me nani does use all dem ripe-ripe banana fuh mek **gulgulah**.*

My grandmother uses all the over-ripe bananas to make **gulgulah**.

gun /gʌn/

will, shall (future tense marker)

Example: *De bassman seh he **gun** cut abee money if abee do wrang-wuk.*

The boss said that he **will** cut our pay if we do a poor job.

gutney /gʊtniː/

wooden utensil used to stir split peas

Example: *Dem big-shat people does use blendah instead ah **gutney** fuh goatay dhal.*

Show off folks use a blender rather than a **gutney** to stir dhal.

gyaaf /gyˈaɪæf/

two or more persons having a conversation

Example: *Every aftnoon dem man dah does siddung bridge canah an **gyaaf**.*

     Every afternoon those men sit by the bridge and **talk.**

gyandaz /gjaɪndaz/

jaundice

Example: *Ah pickney skin yalla-yalla so abee know e get **gyandaz**.*

     The baby's skin was so yellow that we knew it had **jaundice**.

H h

haadluck /hɑ:dlʌk/

not lucky; unfortunate

Example: *Some people get **haadluck** likka dem craas.*

       Some people are so **unfortunate**, it is as if they were cursed.

haalout /h'ɑ:laʊt/

set out

Example: *Ah cane-cuttah tell e wife fah **haalout** e eat.*

       The canecutter told his wife to **set out** his meal.

haal yuh raass /hɑ:l yʊ rɑ:s/

get out (harsh)

Example: *Dah man so rich an religious, but wen wan begga-man show up at e gate e tell de poor man fuh **haal he rass**.*

       That man is so rich and religious, but when a poor man shows up at his gate begging for alms, he tells the poor man to **get out**

haan /h'ɑ:n/

generic name for the entire arm

Example: *Ah baby fall dung an bruise e **haan**.*

       The baby fell and bruised its **arm**.

haan-wash-haan-mek-haan-clean /hˈɑːn-wˈɑːʃ-hˈɑːn-mˈɛk-hˈɑːn-klˈiːn/

to co-operate

Example: *Dem guh do good fuh rememba dat **haan-wash-haan-mek-haan-clean**.*

They had better remember that if **they help us, we will help them**

haat /hˈɑːt/

to hurt

Example: *She does always complain dat she back ah **haat** bad-bad.*

She always complains that her back is **hurting** her.

hag-hair /hˈɑːg-hˈer/

in-grown eyelash

Example: *Me get **hag-hair** in meh eye, so meh nah see too good.*

I have an **in-grown eyelash**, so I can't see well.

hais /hˈaɪs/

to lift, hoist

Example: *Ah baby nah stap cry till e mooma **hais** am.*

The baby does not stop crying until its mother **lifts** it up.

halwah /hɑlwɑ/

a sweet dish of flour and ginger

Example: *Dem Hindu people does mek* **halwah** *fuh baby nine-day.*

Hindus make **a sweet dish of flour and ginger** for a baby's nine-day celebration.

hambug /hˈɑmbʌg/

cause interference

Example: *Me hate wen people* **hambug** *me wen me ah wuk.*

I hate when people **interrupt** me when I am working.

hard ears /hˈɑːd-ˈez/

stubborn; a disobedient person

Example: *Dem chirrun dah so* **hard ears** *dat dem don't listen to nobady.*

Those children are so **stubborn** that they obey no one.

hard-mout /hˈɑːd-mˈaʊt/

mouthy; stubborn

Example: *Da lil gyaal* **hard-mout** *an does even ansa back she own daady.*

That little girl is so **mouthy** that she even rebels against her father.

haslee /hˈɑsli:/

pain in an infant's neck caused by holding it wrongly

Example: *If yuh nah hol ah baby head good, yuh guh gee am **haslee**.*

If you do not hold the baby's head steady, you will cause a **pain in the neck**.

hassar /hˈɑsɑ:/

popular heavily shelled fish

Example: ***Hassar** does taste good-good wen yuh curry am with lil green mango.*

Hassar is delicious when curried with pieces of green mango.

hat-mout /hˈɑt-mˈaʊt/

mouthy

Example: *Dah gyaal ah wan real **hat-mout**, so nah try trubble am.*

That girl is mouthy, so do not try flirting with her.

haul-me-eat /hɑ:-mɪ-i:t/

set out my meal

Example: *Ah bai halla loud-loud fuh he mooma fuh **haul-he-eat**.*

The boy yelled out loudly for his mother to **set out his meal**.

hen don' crow /hɛn do:n kro/

females should not whistle

Example: *Wen me sistah does whisle, me daady does tell she dat **hen don' crow**.*

When my sister whistles, my father tells her that **hens do not crow.**

heng-yuh-mout-weh-sup-ah-leak /hɛŋ-jʌ-maʊt-wɛ-sʌp-a-li:k/

to take advantage of anyone/circumstance for self-benefit

Example: *Nuff people does **heng-dem-mout-weh-sup-ah-leak**.*

Lots of folks **use others for selfish ends.**

he-seh-she-seh /hi:sɛ-ʃi-sɛ/

gossip; second-hand information; hearsay

Example: *Me nah able wid dem people dah **he-seh-she-seh**.*

I cannot tolerate those people's **gossip.**

hooman-cuss /hʌman-kʌs/

menstruation

Example: *Wen dem gyaal get dem mens, dem ol bai does taak bout how dem get **hooman-cuss**.*

When the girls have their periods, the old men refer to it as **women's curse.**

how-de-sun-settin /hɑʊ-di:-sʌn-sɛtɪn/

what time is it?

Example: *Me fren aks me **how-de-sun-setting**, an me tell e de time.*

My friend asked me how-de-sun-setting, so I told him **the time.**

hulko /hˈʌlkɔ/

dried coconut husk

Example: *De ol man complain dat de bread tase like cocnut **huks.***

The old man complained that the bread tasted like coconut **husk.**

hungish /hˈʌɟɪʃ/

greedy

Example: *Some people does guh wedding house an eat like dem **hungish**.*

Some folks go to weddings and eat as if they were **greedy.**

I i

itate /ɑi-teːt/

understand

Example:

*Meh had fuh explain fine-fine before she **itate** wah meh seh.*

I had to explain in fine detail before she could **understand** what I was saying.

J j

jabrey /dʒ'ɑbri/

untidy female

Example: *She mooma seh dat she wary taak to dah gyaal, but she still jabrey-jabrey.*

Her mother said that she was weary talking to her daughter, but she remains an **untidy girl**.

jacketwalah /dʒˌɑkɪtw'ɑːlɑ/

someone who is always in a suit

Example: *All dem school pickney does call de principal **jacketwalah** becaas he does always wear wan suit.*

The school children call the principal **jackeywalah** because he always wears a suit.

jail-bait /dʒ'ɑɪl-b'ɑɪt/

under-aged female

Example: *De ol man warn we not to trouble dah gyaal becaas she ah wan **jail-bait**.*

The old man warned us not to flirt with that girl because she is **under-aged**.

jamrah /dʒˈamrɑ/

frame on which vines grow

Example: *Neighba Seon buil wan **jamrah** fuh grow bora.*

Neighbor Seon built a **frame** on which his bora peas will grow.

jankelar /dʒˈaʃkɛlɑr/

careless

Example: *Harry too damn **jankelar** fuh do he homewuk.*

Harry is too **careless** to do his homework.

jaray /dʒˈɑːreɪ/

curative ritual involving chanting and blowing

Example: *Dem bin kyer ah ol lady to wan pandit fuh **jaray** am, but ah lady dead.*

They took the old lady to a pundit **to cure** her, but she died anyway.

jelaybee /dʒˈɛlaɪbˌiː/

a sweet, coil-like desert/snack

Example: *Me maamy buy five **jelaybee** from de sweetie lady.*

My mother bought five **jelaybee** from the woman who sells sweets.

jhaat /dʒˈɑːt/

pubic hair

Example: *De bai tell abee dat dah bad hooman get nuff-nuff **jhaat**.*

The boy reported to us that the prostitute has lots of **pubic hair**.

jiggah /dʒˈɪɡɑ/

a worm that penetrates the skin

Example: *De bush-dactah dig out ah **jiggah** from e foot.*

The bush-doctor dug out a **worm** from the sole of his feet.

jug /dʒʌɡ/

to reprimand

Example: *De teecha **jug** de bai wen e staat badda dem addah pickney dem.*

The teacher **reprimanded** the boy when he began to interfere with the other students.

juk /dʒˈʌk/

a puncture from a pointed object

Example: *Kelford run barefoot pon ah mud-dam an nail **juk** right through e foot.*

Kelford ran bare footed on the mud street and a nail **went right through** his foot.

juk /dʒˈʌk/

to poke at

Example: *He complain to de teecha dat de other bai juk he wid he haan.*

     He complained to the teacher that the other boy **poked** him with his elbow.

juk /dʒˈʌk/

to outsmart someone

Example: *Sarah juk she fren dem an tell dem she bruks.*

     Sarah **outsmarted** her friends by claiming that she had no money.

juk /dʒˈʌk/

to have sexual intercourse with someone

Example: *Robert boas-up dat e done juk dah gyaal.*

     Robert boasted that he already had **intercourse** with that girl.

juk-dung /dʒʌk-dʊŋ/

a stave

Example: *De crachety lady seh dat de juk-dung knack dung.*

     The quarrelsome woman said that the **surveyor's stave** fell.

jumbie /dʒˈʌmbi/

supernatural being; spirit of a dead person

Example: *Every night da ol lady does frekkin abee wid she jumbie story.*

Every night the old woman scares us with her stories about **supernatural beings**.

jumbie ambrella / dʒˈʌmbi ambrɛla/

mushrooms

Example: *Dem people nah believe me wen me tell dem dat outside people does eat jumbie-amrella.*

The folks did not believe me when I told them that people in other countries eat **mushrooms**.

jun-jun-ee /dʒʌn-dʒʌn-i/

pins and needles, tingling sensation

Examples: *Mary lie dung in de hammock long-long till she foot get jun-jun-ee.*

Mary lay down in the hammock for such a long time that she had **pins and needles** in her feet.

jutah /dʒˈuːtˈɑː/

to taste food or beverage and leave it

Example: *Dah gyaal eat an lef she jutah food just suh.*

That girl ate and left her **half-eaten food** just so.

jutaray /dʒˈuːtˈɑːrˌe/

remnants of food that someone else has eaten

Example: *Me husban does refuse fuh eat **jutaray** food.*

      My husband refuses to eat someone else's **half-eaten** food.

K k

kaasee /kˈɑːsiː/

a type of unscaled fish

Example: *Dem does fine nuff-nuff **kaasee** in ah punt trench.*

They always find lots of that **unscaled fish** in the waterway where sugarcane is loaded into punts.

kabakali /kɑbɑkɑli/

a type of wood

Example: *Dem two young marrid couple mek wan nice-nice lil house wid **kabakali** wood.*

The young married couple made a lovely little house using **kabakali** wood.

kack-up /kɑk-ʌp/

someone who does a bad job

Example: *Nuff-nuff ah dem scamp-man does do sheer **kack-up** wuk, but dem call demself contractah.*

Many of those scampish men do **very bad work**, but they call themselves contractors.

kagaj /kɑːgɑdʒ/

certificate

Example: *Me daady done tell meh dat experience alone nah wuk, meh must get **kagaj** tuh.*

My father told me that experience alone is not enough; it must be backed up by **certified training**.

kaie /kˈai/

algae

Example: *Dem kangcrete in ah yaad full wid **kaie** an people can slip pan am.*

                Their concreted yard has **algae** that make people slip and fall.

kaie /kˈai/

Amerindian spirit

Example: *Sometime he does behave like e get **kaie** pan am.*

                Sometimes he seems to be possessed by **a spirit.**

kaka-hole /kˈɑkɑ-hˈoːl/

anus

Example: *Ah lady tell she data dat she tek she **kaka-hole** an pass she.*

                The woman told her daughter that she **disrespected** her.

kakan /kˈɑkɑn/

celebration on day after a Hindu wedding

Example: *Dem does drink up an fight wen **kakan** day come.*

                They get drunk and brawl on the **day after the wedding**.

kalbalai /kˈɑlbɑlaɪ/

grumbling in the stomach

Example: *Ah man just done eat an he belly still ah*
                   kalbalai *loud-loud.*

                   The man just ate, but his stomach is still
                   grumbling loudly.

kalongie /kalʌndʒi/

stuffed bitter gourd

Example: *Wen me mooma cook dhal, she does mek*
                   kalongie.

                   When my mother cooks dhal, she also
                   makes **stuffed bitter gourd**.

kanaree /kɑnɑːri/

round-bottomed cooking utensil

Example: *All dem house hey get **kanaree** fuh fry ting.*

                   All these homes have **round-bottomed
                   pots** in which they fry foods.

kanchi /kˈantʃi/

small amount

Example: *Me does just put wan **kanchi** saal in meh*
                   food.

                   I put only a **pinch** of salt in my food.

kangalang /kˈɑ̃ɟgɑlˌɑ̃ɟ/

small in size; stunted in growth

Example: *Dem call dah haas wan champyan, but wan*
kangalang haas beat am.

They call that horse a champion, but he
was beaten by a **small** horse.

kanggan /kˈɑ̃ɟgɑn/

celebration on day after a Hindu wedding

Example: *On kanggan day, dem man does pick up*
dem licka an staat fuh fight.

On **the day after the wedding**, the men
drink and begin to fight.

kangkawah /kˈɑ̃ɟkɑwə/

a diamond-shaped kite

Example: *Nuff people nowadays like fuh fly*
kangkawah kite fuh Easter.

Many people these days prefer to fly the
diamond-shaped kite during Easter.

kankce /kˈɑns/

to hit

Example: *He kankce de poor lil bai pon e head haad-*
haad.

He **hit** the little boy on his head.

kankee /kˈɔʃ̬ki:/

sweet dish of pumpkin, cornmeal, coconut steamed in banana leaf

Example: *De best **kankee** me evah eat come pan Machester village on the Corentyne.*

The best **conkie** is made in Manchester village on the Corentyne.

kanwah /kˈɑnwɑ/

cross eyed

Example: *All badee does laff da politician **kanwah** eye.*

Everyone mocks the politician because of his **crossed eyes**.

kanwah-juks /kˈɑnwɑ-dʒˈʌks/

stupid person

Example: *Dah bai ah wan real **kanwah-juks** becaas he does get way fan school.*

That boy is **stupid** because he gets away from school.

karahee /kˈɑrɑːhˌi:/

round-bottomed cooking utensil

Example: *Me mooma does fry she pungkin in wan big **karahee**.*

My mother fries her pumpkin in a big **round-bottom pot**.

karaillah /kˈɑrɑɪlɑ/

bitter gourd

Example: *Dactah tell me dat **karaillah** good fuh blood sugah.*

The doctor told me that **bitter gourd** is good for diabetes.

karaow /kˈɑrˌɑʊ/

type of edible bird

Example: *Dem man does shoot nuff-nuff **karaow** ah backdam.*

The men shoot many **birds** behind the rice fields.

karayjah /kˈɑredʒɑ/

internal organ

Example: *Me wife does always seh she **karayjah** ah hat am.*

My wife always complains that her **insides** hurt.

katchay /kˈɑtʃe/

to wipe a plate clean using hands

Example: *Ah gyaal **katchay** she plate wen she done eat she mango sour an plantain chips.*

The girl **used her hands to wipe her plate clean** after having eaten her plantain chips and mango sour.

katch-katch /kˈatʃ-kˈatʃ/

to nag

Example: Me nevah see wan hooman **katch-katch** like dah wan.

I have never heard a woman **nag** as that woman does.

katch-katch-chai /kˈatʃ-kˈatʃ-tʃˈaɪ/

to nag constantly

Example: Dah gyaal mek ah man lef am wid all she **katch-katch-chai**.

That woman forced the man to leave her because of her **constant nagging.**

kinah /kˈɪnɑ/

to dislike; to scorn

Example: Me wus **kinah** ah fuh see people put dem wet glass jus suh pan ah table.

I **dislike** seeing water from wet glasses on my table.

kiskadee /kˈɪskadˌi:/

a yellow and black bird

Example: Dem **kiskadee** does always mek dem nest in abee guttah.

The **kiskadee birds** always build their nests in our gutter.

kiss-meh-ass /kɪs-mɪ-ɑːs/

go to hell

Example: *Wen ah lady big-big son come beg she fuh money, she tell am fuh go **kiss-she-ass.***

When the woman's adult son begged her for money, she told him to **go to hell.**

kitchree /kˈɪtʃriː/

a dish of rice, split peas and coconut milk

Example: *Leela only know fuh mek **kitchree.***

The only thing that Leela can cook is a **dish of peas and rice.**

kog /koːg/

a Christmas drink of blended milk and raw eggs

Example: *Wen we was lil, we maamy use to gee we **kog** every Christmas.*

When we were young, our mother gave us **egg-nog** every Christmas.

kochar /kˈoːtʃɑr/

sweet talk

Example: *Dah bai tink he ah wan sweet-man an try **kochar** me fuh go wid he.*

That boy thinks he is charming, and he tried to **sweet talk** me into going with him.

kookrit /kˈʌkrɪt/

a thin-fleshed type of fruit with hard cap and skin

Example: *De bes **kookrit** come from Orealla.*

The sweetest **kookerit** fruit comes from Orealla.

koonoo-moonoo /kˈʌːnu-mˈʌnuː/

easily led person

Example: *Dah man wife does treat am like he ah wan real **koonoo-moonoo**.*

That man's wife **bosses him around**.

kootchee /kˈʌtʃiː/

baby talk

Example: *Me aantee pinch meh baby mout an call am **kootchee-kootchee**-koo.*

My aunty pinched my baby's cheeks and **baby talked** with him.

korhi /kˈoːrhi/

a lazy, careless person

Example: *Ah lady does seh dat she dat-in-law ah wan real **korhi**.*

The woman says that her daughter-in-law is **a lazy person**.

kowah /kˈoɑ/

large jackfruit

Example: *We buy wan big **kowah** at Port Mourant maakit las Sataday.*

We bought a very large **jackfruit** at the Port Mourant market last Saturday.

kreketeh /krˈɛkɛt'ɛ/

snail

Example: *Dah rum-shap does mek prapah **kreketeh.***

That bar prepares excellent **snails.**

kreketeh-eatah /krˈɛkɛt'ɛ-ˈiːt'aː/

type of bird that feeds on snails

Example: *Dah **kreketeh-eater** does siddung pon ah wiyah an den fly dung an snatch kreketeh fan ah drainah.*

That **snail-eating bird** sits on the electrical wire, then flies down and gets snails from the drain.

kufum /kʌfʌm/

type of scaled fish

Example: *Abee nah gee abee pickney dem **kufum** fuh eat becaas dah fish get nuff-nuff bone.*

We do not give our children **kufum** to eat because that fish has lots of bones.

kufum /kʌfʌm/

a game played in water

Example: *Dem lil bai does play **kufum** in de trench an hit mattee wid dem foot.*

Those boys play **kufum** in the stream and hit each other with their legs.

kuk kuk beh /kˈʌk kˈʌk bɛ/

severe skin infection

Example: *Ah lady get **kuk-kuk-beh** an people scaan fuh guh near she.*

That woman suffers from **a severe skin infection** causing people to keep away from her.

kungguh-fish /kˈʌɧgʌ-fˈɪʃ/

type of scaled fish

Example: ***Kungguh-fish** look just likka tilapia but e mo lil.*

Kungguh-fish resembles the tilapia fish, but it is smaller.

kuraas /kʊrrɑ:s/

type of unscaled fish

Example: *Nuff-nuff people mout does swell-up wen dem eat **kurass**.*

Many people are allergic to the **kurass** fish.

kyaan-pick-ah-peppah /kyaan-pɪk-a-pɛpʌ/

no luck

Example: *Aftah he lass all e money pon bettin haas, meh uncle complain dat he **kyaan-pick-ah-peppah**.*

After he lost all his money on horse racing, my uncle complained that he has **no luck at all**.

kyaant /ky'a:nt/

to tilt

Example: *Dah house ol-ol, suh he **kyaant** fuh wan-side.*

That house is so old that it is **tilted**.

kyaaten-bail /kyatn̩-baɪl/

a boil on the eye lid

Example: *Dem seh dat if yuh gee somebady someting an yuh tek am back, yuh guh get **kyaaten-bail**.*

They say that if you give something to someone and you take it back, you will have **boils on your eyelid**.

kyat-eye /kʏat-aɪ/

a person with light-coloured eyes

Example: *Hardat like he does see through dem kyaad wid e **kyat-eye**.*

Hardat seems to see through the cards with his **light-eyes**.

L l

laata-dung /le:tə-dʌŋ/

later

Example: *Me tell meh fren dem dat me guh meet dem laata-dung.*

I told my friends that I will meet them **later**.

labar /l'ɑbɑːr/

slow, untidy, careless work/person

Example: *Dah gyaal does do house-wuk labar-labar.*

That girl does housework **untidily.**

labba /lɑbə/

large edible rodent

Example: *We Guyanese does seh dat wen yuh eat labba an drink black water, yuh guh always come back ah Guyana.*

We Guyanese believe that when you eat **labba** and drink black creek water, you will always return home to Guyana.

lack-aff /lɑk-af/

cramp

Example: Haaf way in ah mile-race, e muscle lack-aff.

In the middle of the mile race, he had a cramp.

laddo-gaddo /lˈɑdo-gˈɑdo/

expression equivalent to Lord God

Example: *E fren dead an lef e pickney dem, but e cousin staat waan cry an seh "Oh **laddo-gaddo**, me nah able wid dem problem dis".*

His friend died and left many children, but his cousin whined: **"O Lord-God**, I am unable to deal with these problems"

lagoo-bagoo /lˈɑgu:-bˈɑgu:/

worthless person; idle person

Example: *Sheer **lagoo-bagoo** does deh road-canah night time.*

Only **worthless people** stand around by the road at night.

lampi-pampi /lˈɑmpi-pˈɑ:mpi/

ugly; substandard

Example: *Nuff-nuff people does mek **lampi-pampi** furnitcha.*

Many people make **sub-standard** furniture.

lamutah /lɑmʌtɑ/

a child's stunted growth

Example: *Dem seh dah bai **lamutah** becaas e nah grow.*

They say that the boy is **stunted in his growth**.

lamutah /lɑmʌtɑ/

worthless person

Example: *Dah man does wuk haad-haad, but e son
too **lamutah.***

That man works very hard, but his son is
very **lazy.**

lang belly /lˈaŋ bˈɛlɪ/

a gluttonous person

Example: *E bring all e **lang-belly** fren dem fuh eat
abee weddin-house food.*

He brought all his **gluttonous** friends to eat
at our wedding.

lang-mouth /lˈaŋ-mˈaʊt/

to show displeasure or anger

Example: *Ah gyaal does put on waan **lang-mout** wen
she nah get she own way.*

She shows her **anger** when she does not
get what she wants.

lang-tail hassar /lˈaŋ-tˈeɪl hˈasɑ/

a type of hard-shelled fish

Example: *Me uncle ketch nuff-nuff **lang-tail hassar**
near ah rice field.*

My uncle caught many **long-tail hassar**
fish by the rice field.

lang-wata /lˈaɟ-wˈatˈaː/

tasteless dish

Example: *He complain dat e wife does always mek lang-wata curry.*

He always complains that his wife makes a **tasteless** curry.

lantan-post /lˈantan-pˈoːs/

utility pole

Example: *Ah car lick ah lantan-post an bruk am in two.*

The car hit the **electrical post** and broke it in two.

lapaytay /lˈapeːte/

to spread thickly

Example: *E wife gat fih lapaytay butta pan a bread before e eat am.*

His wife must **spread** butter **thickly** on the bread before he eats it.

lap-clath /lˈapklaːt/

sanitary napkin

Example: *Lang-time hooman does use lap-clath wen dem get dem period.*

Women long ago used **cloth** for sanitary napkins when they menstruate.

lapse /lɑpsi/

a sweet dish of flour, sugar, and milk

Example: *Pandit tell abee dat abee gat fih mek **lapse** fuh do dead wuk fuh abee daady.*

The pundit instructed us to make **lapse** for our father's death anniversary.

lapse lapse /lapɔɪ lapɔi/

too soft

Example: *She put ah rice fuh bail lang-lang till e turn **lapse-lapse**.*

She put the rice to boil for such a long time that it became **too soft**.

larwah /lˈɑːrwɑ/

nothing

Example: *Me famlee dem come fram Merica an dem gee me **larwah**.*

My family came from America but gave me **nothing.**

late-aff /letɑːf/

later

Example: *Me try taak to ah man but he tell me fuh taak to e **late-aff**.*

I tried to speak with the man, but he told me to talk to him **later**.

lat-pat /lˈɑt-pˈɑt/

a dried-down curry

Example: *Me mooma does **lat-pat** dem lil-lil fish.*

My mother makes a **dried-down curry** with small fish.

lazat /lˈɑzɑt/

good luck

Example: *Me money get **lazat**; no mattah how much meh spen, ah money nah done.*

My money has **good luck**; regardless of how much I spend, it does not finish.

lef /lɛf/

to leave

Example: *Me tell ah gyaal fuh **lef** dem wares but e still do am.*

I told the girl to **leave** the dishes, but she still washed them.

lef /lɛf/

to neglect

Example: *Dah nasty gyaal **lef** ah man an she pickney dem an run aff wid she sweet-man.*

That awful girl **abandoned** her husband and children and ran off with her lover.

leh /lɛ/

let; allow

Example:	*Me beg ah gyaal fuh **leh** me go drink wid meh fren dem, but e tell me no.*
	I begged my wife to **allow** me to go with my friends to drink, but she said no.

loh loh /lˈo lˈo/

drool

Example:	*Wen de pickney see e mooma, he does laugh-laugh an **leh-leh** does come down e chin.*
	When the baby sees its mother, he laughs, and **drool** runs down his chin.

likrish /lˈɪkrɪʃ/

greedy

Example:	*Dah man too **lickrish** fa rum.*
	That man is very **greedy** for rum.

lil /lˈɪl/

small

Example:	*Me religious uncle does chase way dem poor beggah-man who does come beg fuh **lil** food.*
	My religious uncle chases away poor beggars who come begging for a **bit** of food.

lime /lˈaɪm/

to hangout, to go to parties frequently

Example: *Dem youtman does **lime** under de ol bus-shed every aftnoon.*

     Those young men **hang out** in the old bus-shed every afternoon.

limsy /lɪmzi:/

bangs

Example: *All she data dem get **limsy** hairstyle.*

     All her daughters have **bangs**.

liva-plate-ah-bun /lɪvɑ-ple:t-ɑ-bʌn/

to be very jealous

Example: *Wen me get up in life, meh aantee **liva-plate-ah-bun**.*

     When I succeed, my aunt becomes **very jealous**.

live-home /lɪv-ho:m/

common-law relationship

Example: *Dem nah marrid; dem does **live home** though.*

     They are not legally married; they **live together** though.

loi /l'o:i:/

dough

Example: *She mix ah **loi** fuh mek bread an lef am fuh raise.*

She mixed the **dough** to make bread and left it to raise.

lolo /l'olo/

penis

Example: *E mooma gat fuh tell da lil bai fuh wash he **lolo** every day.*

His mother must tell the small boy to wash his **penis** every day.

lotay /l'o:t'e/

to dance/gyrate suggestively/drunkenly; to roll around (in mud)

Example: *Me shame-shame how ah gyaal **lotay** sheself front all dem man.*

I was ashamed that the girl **danced drunkenly** in front of all those men.

lowlee /l'o:li:/

penis

Example: *E mooma warn da lil bai fuh wash e **lowlee**.*

His mother waned the little boy to wash his **penis**.

lukanani /lˌuːkɑnˈɑːni/

type of scaled sweet-water fish

Example: *Dah rum shap does mek maastah fry*
lukanani*!*

That rum shop makes masterful fried
lukanani.

luknee /lˈʌkniː/

an elder female charged with ensuring proper contact
between courting/engaged couples

Example: *Me marrid but me nani does still act likka*
*wan **luknee**.*

I am married, but my grandmother still acts
as a **guardian**.

lungarah /lˈʌɟɟeːrɑ/

unemployed, idle person

Example: *Since dah man wife lef am, he turn wan*
*real **lungarah** an ah drink all bout.*

Since that man's wife left him, he became
idle and started drinking everywhere.

lutta /lˈʌtˈɑː/

a skin disease

Example: *Wen me sista eat poke, she does get bad-*
*bad **lutta**.*

When my sister eats pork, she develops
large white blotches on her skin.

M m

maak-a-chodo /mɑ:katʃodo?

a vulgar expression directed against one's mother,
ungrateful

Example: *Dah **maak-a-chodo** bai nah even help e
mooma in she ol age.*

That **ungrateful** boy does not help his aged
mother.

maamee /mˈɑ:mi:/

maternal uncle's wife

Example: *Me **maamee** does fayah she lil shat every
night wen nobady deh.*

My **uncle's wife** takes her drink of liquor
every night when no one is around.

maamee /mˈɑ:mi:/

quince

Example: *Yuh gat fuh peel **maamee** skin before yuh
slice am fuh eat.*

You must peel the skin of the **quince**
before you slice and eat it.

maamoo /mˈɑ:mu/

maternal uncle

Example: *Wen abee bin small, abee **maamoo** use to
beat abee bad-bad wid e belt.*

When we were children, our **mother's
brother** used to beat us severely with his
belt.

maan-kite /mɑːn-kaɪt/

lesbian

Example: *Dem seh dat dah gyaal nice fuh spite but she ah wan **man-kite**.*

They say that that girl is very pretty but that she is a **lesbian**.

mack dactah /mak dɑctah/

quack; ineffective doctor

Example: *Me uncle tink dat me dactah ah wan **mack dactah**.*

My uncle thinks that my doctor is a **quack.**

maga /mˈɑːgɑ/

skinny

Example: *Me waan dah bai dat if e nah eat e food e guh tun **maga-maga**.*

I warned that boy that if he did not eat his food, he will become **very thin**.

maga-daag /mˈɑːgɑ-dˈɑːg/

ungrateful person

Example: *Yuh sarry fuh **maga-daag** an maga-daag tun rung bite yuh.*

You feed **an ungrateful person**, and that person turns on you.

maga-raas /mˈɑːgɑ-rˈɑs/

extremely thin person

Example: *Me uncle tell am fuh kyar e **maga-raas** pon de yaad.*

My uncle told him to take his **skinny self** out of our yard.

main-man /mɛn-mɑ.n/

husband

Example: *Dah wan good woman; she seh she gat she good-good **main-man**, wah she guh do wid some lungarah.*

That is a good woman; she says that she has a good **husband**, so why would she go with a wastrel.

mamagai /mɑmɑgˌaɪ/

to lie or trick someone

Example: *E does call eself businessman, but e does **mamagai** allbady.*

He calls himself a businessman, but he **cheats** everyone.

mangro /mɑːŋgroː/

mango

Example: *De best **mangro** is black spice **mangro**.*

The best **mango** is black spice **mango.**

manish /mˈɑnɪʃ/

wicked; willful

Example: *Dah **manish** lil bai does always get way pan school.*

      That **wicked** boy always gets away from school.

marabunta /mˈɑrɪbʌntɑ/

wasp

Example: ***Marabunta** bite Kelford pan he lip an e lip swell up big-big.*

      A **wasp** stung Kelford on his lip and it was badly swollen.

marsaray /mɑːrsɑrˌe/

to inflict serious injury

Example: *Me daady tell am seh e guh **marsaray** am if e come back ah abee shap.*

      My father told him that he would give him **a good thrashing** if he came back to our shop.

marsaray-yuh-beef /mɑːrsɑrˌe-jʌ-biːf/

to inflict serious injury or death

Example: *Me daady tell am seh e guh **marsaray e beef** if e come back ah abee shap.*

      My father told him that he would give him **a good thrashing** if he came back to our shop.

masala /mɑsɑlɑ/

spices used to cook

Example: *Dem seh dat dem Chinee does cook curry widdout* **masala**.

They say that the Chinese cook curry without using **masala**.

mash /mˈɑʃ/

celebration commemorating Guyana's Republic Day

Example: *We does celebrate* **Mash** *on Febuary 23.*

We celebrate **Mashramani** on February 23.

matchan /mˈatʃɑn/

an erected frame upon which vines grow

Example: *Dem faamah mek* **matchan** *fuh dem bora run pan.*

The farmers built **frames** for their bora vines to grow on.

matee /mˈatˈiː/

friend

Example: *Me mooma seh right aff dat me an she nah* **matee.**

My mother was clear that she and I were not **pals**.

mauby /mɔbi/

a drink made from the bark of a tree

Example: *Fraser maamee use to mek champian*
                    mauby.

                    Fraser's mother made excellent mauby
                    drink.

mausi /mʌsi:/

maternal aunt

Example: *Me **mausi** dead las week an me miss am*
                    bad-bad.

                    My **aunt** died last week, and I miss her
                    terribly.

meh /m'ɪ/

me; my

Example: *She seh dat she nah able tek an **meh***
                    worries.

                    She said that she cannot take on **my**
                    troubles.

meh buddy pickney /mɪ bʌdi pɪknɛ/

my brother's child

Example: ***Meh buddy pickney** seh e waan guh UG.*

                    My brother's son said that he wanted to
                    attend the University of Guyana.

meh sissy pickney /mɪ sisi pɪknɛ/

my sister's child

Example: ***Meh sissy pickney** seh she just waan marrid an mek pickney.*

My sister's daughter said that she just wants to get married and have babies.

mek /mɛk/

make

Example: *He wan good-good bai, but e fren dem **mek** e tun suh.*

He is a good boy, but his friends **made** him become bad.

mek-bassa-bassa /mɛk-bɑsɑ-bɑsɑ/

waste time; create confusion

Example: *Every time abee get jhandi, dah lady does come **mek** nuff-nuff **bassa-bassa**.*

Every time we have a religious function, that woman comes and **creates** great **confusion**.

metche-metche /mˈɛtʃɛ-mˈɛtʃɛ/

tasteless and numerous home decorations; clutter

Example: *Me wife does dress up abee house wid sheer **metche-metche**.*

My wife decorates our home with **tasteless clutter**.

metemjee /mˈɛtˈɛm:dʒˈiː/

 dried-down dish of provisions

Example: *Me aantee laff me becaas me mek*
                 ***metemjee** widdout duff.*

                 My aunt laughed at me because I made
                 dried down provisions without dumplings.

money-guh-weh-money-deh /mʌni-gʌ-wɛ-mʌni-dɛ/

the rich get richer; money attracts money

Example: *Me daady binna always tell me dat **money***
                 ***guh-weh-money-deh**.*

                 My father always tells me that **money
                 attracts money**.

monkey /mˈʌɟki/

heavy, two-handled tool used to drive wooden staves into
the ground

Example: *Dem two bai use wan **monkey** fuh hammah*
                 down ah pos in ah grung.

                 The two boys used a **two-handle ram** to
                 drive the post into the ground.

monkey face bleedin /mˈʌɟki fes bliːdən/

menstruation

Example: *He tell abee dat pon e weddin night, e wife*
                 *tell am seh nuttin fuh he cas **monkey face***
                 ***bleedin**.*

                 He told us that on his wedding night his
                 wife told him there will be no sex because
                 she had her **period**.

moolah /mu:lɑ/

money

Example: *Me son seh he guh invite all e fren dem becaas e get nuff **moolah**.*

My son told me that he will invite all his friends because he has lots of **money.**

mooma /mˈu:mɑ/

mother

Example: *Me mout fall open wen me hear ah bai call e **mooma,** "Mother".*

I was agape when the boy called his **mother**, "Mother".

mooma-rass /mˈu:mɑ-rˈɑ:s/

vulgar expression referring to someone's mother's behind

Example: *Wen he aks fuh money, e mooma tell am fuh haul e **mooma-raas**.*

When he asked for money, his mother told him to **get lost**.

moongazah /mˈu:ngæzɑ/

supernatural being; human-like but very tall

Example: *Me daady swear seh he see wan **moongazah**.*

My father swore that he saw **a supernatural being**.

moon-pass /mˈuːn-pˈɑːs/

old; infertile

Example: *Me tell meh fifty-five year ol mamoo dat he bettah marrid quick before he come **moon-pass**.*

I told my fifty-five-year-old uncle that he had better get married quickly before he gets **too old to have children**.

moreish /morɪʃ/

food that is worthy of having another helping

Example: *Dis food tase good-good till e tase **moreish**.*

This food tastes so delicious that it is **worthy of another helping**.

mosah /mˈɔːsɑ/

maternal aunt's husband

Example: *Me **mosah** buy new kyar and he staat waan show aff wid heself.*

My **uncle** bought a new car and suddenly started to show off.

mother-sally /mʌdɑ-sɑli/

tall female figure paraded during festive seasons

Example: *Evry Christmas we does get **mother sally** come down Duncan Street wid masquerade.*

Every Christmas we would have **mother-sally** coming down Duncan Street with the masquerade.

mout /maʊt/

to argue

Example: *Ah lil bai **mout** ah teecha wen she bin aks fuh e homewuk.*

The little boy **argued** with the teacher when she asked for his homework

muk /mˈʌlʊ/

a stupid or foolish person

Example: *Dah scamp-man try sell me fake gold like me is a **muk**.*

That scamp tried selling me fake gold as if I was a **stupid person.**

muscle-bung /mʌsl̩-bʌŋ/

muscular pain, cramp

Example: *Abee staat exercise Monday, an by Tuesday evrybady gat **muscle-bung**.*

We began exercising on Monday, but by Tuesday we all had **muscle pains.**

muzzee /mˈʌziː/

maybe, perhaps

Example: *Aunty Rita seh dat Uncle Basil nah deh home, e **muzzee** gaan rum shap.*

Aunty Rita said that Uncle Basil was not home, that he **perhaps** went to the bar.

N n

nack /nˈɑːk/

to hit

Example: *E **nack** e buddy an catch fayah pon e mooma.*

He **hit** his brother and got punished by his mother.

nack /nˈɑːk/

to have intercourse

Example: *Ah bai bose dat e done **nack** dah gyaal.*

The boy boasted that he **had intercourse** with that girl.

nackabout /nɑkabˌaʊt/

idle, restless person

Example: *Aftah he laas e jab, me daady tun wan real **nackabout.***

After my father lost his job, he became **idle**.

nackabout /nɑkabˌaʊt/

loose woman

Example: *Abee kyaan believe e marrid dah **nackabout** lady.*

We cannot believe that he got married to that **loose** woman.

nack-knee /nˈɑk-nˈiː/

both knees bent inward

Example: *Dem does prapah laff ah bai becaas e get nack-knee.*

        They really mock the boy because his legs were **misshapen at the knees**.

nah /nˈɑː/

no, not

Example: *Me nah guh wid ayuh fuh lime ah rum-shap.*

        I am **not** going with you to hang out at the bar.

nah-easy /nɑːiːzi/

hard to deal with, harsh, humorous

Example: *Dem bai seh dat dem baas-man nah-easy.*

        The boys said that their boss is very **harsh**.

nana /nˈɑːnɑ/

maternal grandfather

Example: *Me mooma seh dat nana bin look afta she wen she bin lil-lil.*

        My mother said that my **grandfather** cared for her when she was a little girl.

nani /nˈɑːni/

maternal grandmother

Example: *Ah gyaal like she **nani** mo dan e like e own mooma.*

The girl loved her **grandmother** more than she loved her own mother.

nara /nˈɑːrɑ/

stomach ache

Example: *Ah man seh e get **nara** after e fetch wan whole bag rice.*

The man said he had a **stomach pain** after carrying a full bag of rice.

nata-batee /nɑtɑ-bɑti/

worthless, pretentious person

Example: *Dah man ah wan **nata-batee** but he like press up heself.*

That man is a **worthless fool** who likes to inflate himself.

ne'er-do-well /nˈer-dʌ-wˈɛl/

a person who never does well

Example: *She spail ah bai suh much dat he come wan **ne'er-do-well**.*

She spoiled the boy so much that he became **worthless**.

necklee /nˈɛkliː/

small scaled fresh-water fish

Example: *Dem tung people does call kokabelly* **necklee***.*

The Georgetown folk call the coocoohellce fish by the name of **necklee**.

neemakaram /nˈiːmak̚ˌaram/

ungrateful person

Example: *Dah **neemakaram** bai teef ah poor lady money aftah she cook an feed am.*

That **ungrateful** scamp stole the poor woman's money after she cooked and fed him.

nenwah /nˈɛnwɑ/

fresh sponge gourd; lufa

Example: *Dem foreigna does use **nenwah** fuh scrub dem skin.*

Foreigners use **lufa** to bathe.

neva-see-come-fuh-see /nˈɛvə-siː-kʌm-fʌ-siː/

one who goes to others' homes and mimics behaviors and things

Example: *She come hey an watch me pickney clothes an tays likka wan real **neva-see-come-fuh-see.***

She comes to our home and eyes my child's clothes and toys **to buy the same** things for her child.

neva-see-come-fuh-see /nˈɛvə-siː-kʌm-fʌ-siː/

one who is boastful of possessing ordinary things

Example: *She get like wan real **neva-see-come-fuh-see** wen she husban buy wan ol-ol secand-hand kyaar.*

She became boastful after she and her husband bought an old second-hand car.

new-brain /nˈuː-brˈen/

an illiterate person

Example: *Me driva does puff up heself, but he ah wan real **new-brain**.*

My driver is an arrogant fellow, but he is illiterate.

nose-cold /nˈoːz-kˈoːl/

a leak from the nostrils; booger

Example: *Me get flu, an meh **nose-cold** ah run likka pipe.*

I have the flu, and my **nose is as runny** as a tap.

nose-hole /nˈoːz-hˈoːl/

nostrils

Example: *Ah flu mek meh **nose-hole** clag-up.*

The flu has my **nostrils** blocked.

nuff /nˈʌf/

a lot of something

Example: Dem get **nuff** money but dem ah simple-simple people.

They are **wealthy**, but they remain simple folk.

nuff nuff /nˈʌf-nˈʌf/

excessive amount

Example: Dem get **nuff-nuff** mangro pan dem tree, but dem naah gee nobady waan even.

They have **lots** of mangoes on their trees, but they refuse to give away even one.

nugget /nˈʌgɛt/

generic name for all shoe polish

Example: Daady buy wan Kiwi **nugget** fuh polish meh school shoes.

My dad bought a can of **Kiwi polish** for my school shoes.

nuh /nʌ/

please

Example: E maamy beg ah bai: "Ow, beta, eat **nuh**."

His mother begged the boy to **please** eat.

nyaam /naɪɑ:m/

to eat hurriedly

Example: *Ah bai come home hungry-hungry an*
*   **nyaam** out e food.*

        The boy came home hungry and **ate his**
        food hurriedly.

O o

obeah /ˈobɪɑː/

witchcraft

Example: *Ah gyaal geh sick, so dem seh somebady* ***obeah*** *am.*

The girl got ill, so they concluded that someone **cast a spell** of her.

ole-bai /ˈoːl-bˈaɪ/

elderly man

Example: *Dah* ***ole-bai*** *strang-strang; he only look so weaky-weaky.*

That **old man** is very strong; he only looks fragile.

ole-bai /ˈoːl-bˈaɪ/

father

Example: *Me* ***ole-bai*** *seh dat meh kyaan play cricket till meh done me school wuk.*

My **father** said that I can only play cricket after I have done my homework.

ole-gyaal /ˈoːl-gˈɪɑːl/

elderly woman

Example: *Dah* ***ole-gyaal*** *does weed she yaad by sheself.*

That **elderly woman** weeds her own yard.

ole-gyaal /ˈoːl-gˈɪɑːl/

mother

Example: *Me **ole-gyaal** really strict wid abeedeez.*

       My **mother** is strict with us.

ol higue /ˈoːl ˈɑiːg/

supernatural being; living old woman who sheds her skin
and turns into a ball of fire; sucks blood of sleeping
children

Example: *Maanin time, me see big-big bite maak pon*
       *meh pickey skin, an me aantee seh dat **ol***
       ***higue** bite am.*

       In the morning I found bite marks on my
       baby, and my aunty was certain that **ol
       higue** had bitten her.

one-one time / wɑn-wɑːn-tɑɪm

sometimes, infrequently

Example: *He does tek e drinks **one-one time**.*

       He takes a few drinks **every now and then**.

one-time /wɑːn-tɑɪm/

right away

Example: *Me mooma tell meh fuh go bade **one-time***
       before meh guh school.

       My mother told me to shower **right away**
       for school.

ouchay /ˈaʊtʃe/

ritual to heal a sick infant

Example: *Ah lady **ouchay** she baby becaas she say
ah baby get bad-eye.*

      The woman tried to cure her sick baby with
a ritual because the child was sick.

outside /aʊts aɪd/

a foreign country

Example: *Nuff-nuff Guyanese spen six mont **outside**
an come back hey fuh show aff.*

      Lots of Guyanese go away for six months
in **America** and return to show off.

ova-duh-de-duh //ovɑ-dʊh-dɛ-du:/

to overindulge

Example: *Wen e wife cuss am in front e fren dem, he
shout pan she dat she ah **ova-duh-de-duh.***

      When his wife swore at him in front of his
friends, he shouted at her that she was
over-doing it.

P p

paglee /pˈɑgliː/

an insane person; a clumsy person

Example: *Dah bai so **paglee** he nah know weh e bak deh an weh e belly deh.*

That boy is so **stupid** that he does not know his back from his front.

pakan /pˈɑkɑn/

to feign unwillingness

Example: *Wen me affah she food, she does always show **pakan**.*

Every time I offer her food, she **pretends** as if she is unwilling to eat.

pakoo /pɑkuː/

one partner cannot control the other: a naive person

Example: *Ayuh tink dat dah bai ah wan **pakoo**, but e mo smaat dan all ayuh.*

All of you think that the boy is **naïve**, but he is smarter than the rest of you.

pall-aff /pˈɑːl-ˈɑf/

wooden siding for waterways to avoid caving in of dirt

Example: *Dah cheap-man mek dem **pall-aff** wid ol wood.*

That stingy man made the **siding of his drain** with old wood.

pallin /pˈɑːlɪn/

wood used to make a wooden siding for waterways to avoid caving in of dirt

Example: *Some people does use kabakali wood fuh mek **pallin**.*

    Some folks use the Kabakali wood for **drain sidings**

palpatai /pɑlpɑtaɪ/

to palpitate

Example: *Wen me see dem police come to meh gate, me heart staat **palpatai** bad-bad.*

    When the police came to my gate, my heart started **to race wildly**.

pampee /pˈɑːmpiː/

kernel of coconut from which sprouts a new coconut plant

Example: *Meh daady fren gee e wan **pampee** cocnut fuh plant in abee backyaad.*

    My father's friend gave him a **coconut kernel** to plant in our backyard.

pampers /pˈɑmpɑz/

generic name for all diaper

Example: *Me hussy buy wan pack huggies **pampas** fuh abee pickney.*

    My husband bought a pack of Huggies **diapers** for our child.

parsad /pˈɑːrsɑːd/

sweet dish of flour, sugar, ghee, and milk

Example: *Abee cook nuff-nuff **parsad** fuh abee jhandi, but dem pickney eat out half.*

We made lots of **parsad** for our religious ceremony, but the children ate half of it.

pashuma /pɑʃumɑ/

a child's stunted growth

Example: *Dem dacta seh dat ah bai **pashuma** becaas e gat bad haat.*

The doctors claimed that the boy is **stunted in growth** because of his heart condition.

pasray /pˈɑsreː/

to sit heavily

Example: *Dah gyaal always does come an **pasray** she backside likka wan elephant.*

That girl always shows up and **flops** on her behind like an elephant.

pasray /pˈɑsreː/

to sit lazily and idly

Example: *Me pay she fuh wuk, but she does just **pasray** an watch dem adda gyaal wuk.*

I pay her to work, but she always just **sits around** and watch the other girls do the work.

patacake /pˈatˈɑːkek/

vagina

Example:　　　*De lil gyaal maamy does always remine she fuh wash she **patacake**.*

The little girl's mother constantly reminds her to wash her **vagina**.

patchaunee /pˈʊtʃaʊnɪː/

curried sheep intestine

Example:　　　*Me granny too like **patchaunee** an dhal.*

My grandmother really likes **curried sheep intestine** and split peas.

patience /pˈeɪʃəns/

solitaire, the card game

Example:　　　*From de time cack crow, da wase-man tek out he deck kyaad an staat play **patience**.*

From the crack of dawn that idle man takes out his deck of cards and starts playing **solitaire.**

patkay /pˈɑtkeɪ/

to toss; to throw down heavily

Example:　　　*Dah gyaal like fuh just **patkay** everything bladam-bladam.*

That girl likes to **throw things down** with a bang.

patsalt /pˈɑtsɑlt/

one who is at each gathering; one who gets into everyone's business

Example: *Dah bai ah wan **patsalt**; everyway yuh turn, he deh-deh mining people business.*

That boy is **always present** at every turn intruding into other people's affairs.

pat-tell-e-matee-e-battam-black /pˈɑt-tˈɛl-ˈiː-mˈɑtˈiː-ˈiː-bˈɑtˈɑm-blˈɑk

to accuse someone else when one is guilty of the same crimes/mistakes

Example: *De man call me schupit, an me tell am seh **pat-ah-tell-e-matee-e-battam-black**.*

The man called me stupid, and I told him he was **equally** as stupid.

patwa /pˈɑtwə/

the name of a flat, scaled fish

Example: *Dem lil bai ketch nuff-nuff **patwa** in ah trench wid hook.*

The young boys caught a lot of **flat, scaled fish** in the pond using fishing hooks.

paylin /peːlɪn/

picket fence

Example: *Me mooma mek wan **paylin** fence fuh stap dem cow fuh eat out she plant dem.*

My mother made a **picket fence** to prevent the cows from eating her plants.

paynoose /pe:nu:s/

a sweet dessert made from post-birth cow's milk and sugar

Example: *Evry time abee cow drap, abee does use ah milk fuh mek* **paynoose***.*

       Every time our cows give birth, we use the milk to make **paynoose.**

paysee /pˈeɪsi:/

a wasp that if infamous for building nests in homes

Example: *Dem* **paysee** *mek nuff-nuff mud nes in abee house.*

       The **wasps** built many mud nests in our home.

paysee-paysee /pˈesi:-pˈesi:/

sticky

Example: *Ah pickney mout* **paysee-paysee** *wen e done eat ah sweetie.*

       The child's mouth was **sticky** after she ate the candy.

peel-neck /pˈil-nˈɛk/

a yard fowl without feathers on the neck

Example: *Meh fren seh dat dem* **peel-neck** *fowl does prapah beat up dem duck an turkey.*

       My friend claims that **her fowl with the featherless neck** beats up on the ducks and turkeys.

pepperpot /pˈɛpɚpˌɑːt/

an indigenous dish of cassareep and meat

Example: *Christmas time plenty people does eat*
pepperpot wid bread.

    During the Christmas season, it is
customary to make **pepperpot** and freshly
baked bread.

phagwah /phɑgwɑ/

a Hindu spring harvest festival also called Holi

Example: *Evry Phagwah me three pickney does come*
back from school wid dem clothes an skin
stain wid red an blue an wid powder in
dem hair.

    Every **Phagwah** my three children return
from school with their clothes and skin
stained with red and blue and with powder
in their hair.

phatkay /patke/

to throw down carelessly

Example: *Every day, meh son does come from school,*
phatkay he schoolbag, and gaan play
cricket.

    Every day, my son returns from school,
throws down his schoolbag, and rushes off
to play cricket.

photo-take-outer /fo:to-tɛkɑʊ-tɑ/

a photographer

Example: *Fuh me data weddin, abee hire wan special*
              ***photo-take-outa** fuh tek pictures.*

              We hired a special **photographer** to take
              out pictures.

pickney /pɪknɪ/

child/children

Example: *Dem **pickey** dah prapah badarashan.*

              Those **children** are troublesome.

pick-up /pɪkʌp/

support or defend someone

Example: *Dah lady does **pick-up** fuh she son even tho*
              she know e wrang-wrang.

              That woman **defends** her son even though
              she knows he has done wrong.

pidgy-wink /pɪdʒi-wɪnk/

hyperactive

Example: *Wen me sistah bring she pickney dem ya,*
              *dem does **pidgy-wink** all ova me house.*

              When my sister brings her children here,
              they **run wild** all over my house.

pimpish /pɪmpɪʃ/

sly observer

Example: *She does play like she nice, but she* ***pimpish***, *mining evrybady business.*

She pretends to be nice, but she **involves** herself in everyone's private affairs.

pinetah-broom /pˈaɪntə-brˈuːm/

broom made from the midrib of coconut leaves

Example: *Aunty Lena seh dat* ***pinetah-broom*** *does sweep ah house battam mo betta dan stick broom.*

Aunty Lena insists that the **broom made from coconut leaves** are better than stick brooms for sweeping the bottom of the house.

pipe /pˈaɪp/

generic name for all faucets or taps

Example: *Ah bai fuhget fuh tun aff ah* ***pipe*** *an water run whole night.*

The boy forgot to turn off the **tap** and the water flowed throughout the night.

piwari /pˈaɪwɑri/

indigenous drink of fermented fruit and vegetable peels

Example: *Me drink nuff-nuff* ***piwari*** *an get suh drunk till me fall dung.*

I drank so much **piwari** that I got drunk and fell.

play /ple:/

to be possessed

Example:	*Dem seh wen dem pandit ah **play**, dem kyan tell yuh yuh futcha.*

Example: *Dem seh wen dem pandit ah **play**, dem kyan tell yuh yuh futcha.*

They claim that when their pundit is possessed, he can tell you your future.

plimplah /pl'ɪmplɑ/

thorn

Example: *Dah gyaal climb-up ah lime tree an **plimplah** juk am all ovah.*

The girl climbed the lime tree and the **thorns** pricked her everywhere.

po-house /p'o:haʊs/

house for the elderly or poverty-stricken

Example: *Me husband does spend money wild-wild, so meh tell he dat abee guh end up in **po-house**.*

My husband spends money so wildly that I had to warn him that we will end up in **a home for poor people**.

pooch-paatch /pu:-pɑ:tɑ:tʃ/

careless or sloppy work

Example: *Dah poor ol lady cry wen she tell abee how she pay nuff-nuff money fuh dem contracta do **pooch-paatch** wuk pon she house.*

That poor old woman wept when she told us how she paid lots of money for the carpenters to do **shoddy** work on her house.

poohar /pˈuːhɑːr/

lazy or careless

Example: *Uncle Seeram seh how he shame dat e data so **poohar** dat she house always nasty-nasty.*

My father always had a **religious ceremony** to celebrate his birthday.

Uncle Seeram said how ashamed he was that his daughter is so **lazy** that her home was always very dirty.

poojah /pˈuːdʒɑ/

Hindu ritual of thanksgiving or commemoration

Example: *Me daady bin always do **poojah** fuh he birdday.*

My father always had a **religious ceremony** to celebrate his birthday.

poonch-paunching /puː-pɑːtɑːtʃɪŋ/

to complete a job in a careless manner

Example: *De bassman warn dem dat he nah guh pay dem fuh dem **pooch-paunching**.*

The boss warned them that he will not pay them for **careless work**.

poopah /pˈuːpɑ/

paternal aunt's husband

Example: *Wen abee had nuttin fuh eat, me **poopah** bin help abee.*

When we had nothing to eat, it was my **aunt's husband** who helped us.

poopsie /pˈʌːpsi/

to pass gas

Example: *Abee had wan good laugh wen me lil baby leggo wan big **poopsie**.*

We had a good laugh when my little baby **passed gas** loudly.

poowah /pˈuːɑ/

paternal aunt

Example: *Wen me **poowah** dead, not even wan ah she pickney dem come from outside fuh bury she.*

When my **father's sister** died, not even one of her children came from abroad for her funeral.

pope /poːp/

to break into a line

Example: *Me buddy does use e lil-lil pickney fuh **pope** de line.*

My brother uses his little child **to get ahead** of the line.

popo /pˈoːpo/

police

Example: *Abee had to call dem **popo** pon abee neighba wen dem threaten abee.*

We had to call the **police** when our neighbor threatened us.

posey /poːzi/

chamber-pot

Example: *Dem ol people get inside tailet, but demma still use **posey** night-time.*

Those old folks have inside washroom, but they still use **chamber-pots** at night.

potagee /pˈʌtˈɑgˌiː/

Portuguese

Example: *Dem **potagee** people does tun red-red wen dem deh in ah sun.*

Portuguese folks turn red when they are in the sun.

poung /pˈʌɟ/

to pound or grind

Example: *All bady had to help me maamee **poung** mango fuh mek achar fuh abee jhandi.*

Everyone had to help my mother to **pound** mango in order to make achar for our religious ceremony.

poung name / pˈʌɟ neːm/

gossip

Example: *As soon as dah gyaal open she big mout, she staat **poung** name.*

As soon as that girl opens her big mouth, she starts to **gossip**.

puckney /pˈʌkni/

pipe-like instrument used to intensify flames in firesides

Example: *Me maamy staat quarrel wid abee wen she kyaan fine she **puckey** fuh light she fireside.*

My mother started to quarrel when she could not find her **instrument** to light her fireside.

pull-meh-eat /pˈʌl-mˈɛ-ˈiːt/

set out a meal

Example: *Dah bai bin Kyanada ten year now, but he still ah tell e mooma **fuh pull he eat**.*

That boy was in Canada for ten years, but he still demands that his mother **set out his meal.**

pulouree /pʊlɑʊrˌiː/

small, round, savory dish mainly of flour and split peas

Example: *Me like eat **pulouree** wid mangro sour.*

I like to eat **pulouri** with mango sour.

pum-pum /pˈʌm-pˈʌm/

vagina

Example: *All dem bai does wait fuh watch ah gyaal becaas she dress so shaat dem can almost see she **pum-pum**.*

All the boys waited to watch that girl because her dress was so short as to show her **privates.**

puri /pu:'ri/

deep-fried flat bread

Example: *Me favorite weddin house food ah **puri** an guruma.*

My favorite wedding house food is **fried flat bread** and sweetened mango curry.

purine-leaf /pu:rɑi:n-l'i:f/

lotus leaf

Example: *Dem people share food in some big-big **purine-leaf** at dem son weddin.*

Those people served food in some big **lotus leaves** at their son's wedding.

purple-heart /pʌrpḷ-hɑrt/

a decorative purple-coloured wood

Example: *Me daady does always use **purple-heart** fuh mek abee furniture.*

My father always used **purple-heart** wood to make our furniture.

pusoor-pusoor /p'ʌsʌ:r-pʌ:sʌ:r/

to gossip

Example: *Me big sista does only wait fuh **pusoor-pussoor** bout people.*

My eldest sister is always anxious to **gossip** about others.

putuh-putuh /pʌtˈʌ-pʌtˈʌ/

very soft mud

Example: *Dem lil bai play big man fuh guh ketch crab, but dem get stick up in de **putuh-putuh mud.***

The young boys acted like big men and went to catch crabs, but they got stuck in the **soft mud**.

Q q

queh-queh /kwˈeɪ-kwˈeɪ/

dances and ceremonies on the wedding eve night

Example: *We does get nuff fun singin an dancing at* **queh-queh**, *but we does larn nuff-nuff tings tuh.*

We have fun singing and dancing at **queh-queh**, but we learn many things as well.

R r

raas /rˈɑːs/

backside

Example:　*Dah bai binna look pon e phone an step pon wan banana skin an fall flat pon e rass.*

That boy was gazing at his phone when he stepped on a banana peel and fell flat on his **backside**.

rajkaray /rˈɑːdʒkɑrˌe/

to live with gay abandon

Example:　*Rajesh jus rajkaray all dah money wa e mooma lef am.*

Rajesh simply **squandered** all the money he inherited from his mother.

rakhee /rɑːkhiː/

ash from fireside used to clean pots and pans

Example:　*Aunty Baby does use rakhee fuh shine all dem pat battam wen she done cook.*

Aunty Baby uses **ash** to clean all her pot bottoms after she cooks.

rakhee /rɑːkhiː/

a string tied around the wrist to signify brotherhood

Example:　*Every Rakhee day me does mek sure me guh see me buddy dem.*

Every **Raksha Bandhan Day** I am sure to visit my brothers.

ramshackle /ramʃakəl/

dilapidated

Example: *Plenty people come together an mek-ova de*
*ol lady **ramshackle** house nice-nice.*

      Many people joined hands and renovated
the old woman's **dilapidated** house into a
nice home.

rap /rˈɑp/

three-card poker game

Example: *Dem Corentyne man dem bin play **brag** fuh*
tree day an tree night.

      Those Corentyne men used to play **three-
card poker** for three days and nights.

rass-pass /rˈɑːs-pˈɑːs/

to disrespect someone

Example: *De man seh dat is sheer **rass-pass** dat e son*
bring e fren dem an drink up in e house.

      The man said that it was sheer **disrespect**
that his son brought his friends and got
drunk in his home.

romaal /rˈoːmɑːl/

women's head-covering' usually plaid of red, black and
white or yellow

Example: *Dem ol time Hindu lady never bin guh out*
*dem house widdout **romaal** pon dem head.*

      Old-time Hindu women never left home
without their **head-covering**.

roti /ɹˈoːtˈiː/

any flat bread

Example: *Me favorite food is chicken curry an **roti**.*

              My favorite dish is chicken curry and **roti**.

rub /rˈʌb/

to wash clothes by hand

Example: *Me granny generation use to **rub** clothes
               trench-side.*

              My grand-mother's generation **washed**
              their clothes by the stream.

rum /rˈʌm/

generic name for all alcoholic beverages

Example: *Me big-shot uncle does only drink Johnny
               Walker **rum**.*

              My big-shot uncle drinks only Johnny
              Walker **scotch**.

run-yuh-mout /rʌn-yʌ-maʊt/

to speak out of turn, gossip

Example: *Me nah tell she nuttin becaas she like **run-
               she-mout**.*

              I do not like telling her anything because
              she gossips.

S s

saal-pass /sˈɑːl-pˈɑːs/

children's game resembling relay

Example: *Dem pickney dese days too busy wid cellphone fuh play game likka **saal-pass**.*

Children these days are too busy with cellphones to play games like **saal-pass**.

saapee /sˈɑːpiː/

pot-cloth

Example: *Aunty Rattie complain dat she dat-in-law does use nasty **saapee** for tek out she pat panna stove.*

Aunty Ratti complained that her daughter-in-law uses a dirty **pot cloth** to take her hot pots off the stove.

sadarin /sˈɑdɑːrɪn/

female overseer of weeders at the sugar estate

Example: *Dah **sadarin** nah even low dem lady weeda fuh drink lil wata in de hat-hat sun.*

That **female overseer** does not allow her female weeders to have a sip of water while they work in the hot sun.

salara /sɑlɑːrɑ/

cake with red coconut filling

Example: *Dem tung people does call **salara** "red cake".*

City people call **salara** by the name "red cake".

salipentah /sˈɑlɪpˌɛntɑ/

long lizard-like reptile

Example: *Neighba does vex bad-bad wen dem*
salipentah does eat out all e fowl egg.

Our neighbor gets angry when the **reptile**
eats his chicken eggs.

salsew /sˈɑːlseʊː/

or chicken foot, made of split peas

Example: *Abee school kyanteen does sell nice salsew*
an tambrin sour.

Our school canteen sells tasty **chicken foot**
and tamarind sour.

samdin /sˈɑmdɪn/

the respective mothers of husband and wife

Example: *All awee suprise how good dem two*
samdin does get alang.

All of us were surprised at how well the
two **mothers-in-law** get along.

sanay /sˈɑːne/

to mix food with fingers

Example: *Wen me sanay meh food, e does taste mo*
sweet.

When I use my **fingers to eat**, my food
tastes better.

saro-bai /sɑ:ro-baɪ/

two men married to two sisters

Example: *Dem two **saro-bai** nah get alang waan bit, but dem does drink evryday togedda.*

Those two **brothers-in-law** do not get along with each other at all, yet they drink with each other every day.

scamp-man /skˈæmp-mˈɑn/

a liar or thief

Example: *Dah whole village full ah **scamp-man**.*

That entire village is full of **thieves and liars**.

scratchetee /skrˈɑtʃətˌi:/

ill-tempered

Example: *Mo ol nana get, de mo **scratchetee** he get.*

The older grandpa gets, the more **irritable** he becomes.

scraven /skrˈe:vən/

gluttonous

Example: *Me son fren dem does eat like dem **scraven**.*

My son's friends eat as if they were **ravenous**.

scraven-guts /skrˈe:vən-gˈʌts/

gluttonous person

Example: *Me warn meh son not fuh bring e **scraven-guts** fren dem home hey.*

I warned my son not to bring his **gluttonous** friends to our home.

see-far /s iː-ɹ ɑːɹ/

a person who can see into the future

Example: *Dah ol man ah wan **see-far** man, so we does listen to he advice.*

That old man can **see into the future**, so we always heed his advice.

seh /sɛ/

that

Example: *People tink **seh** he ah wan bad-man, but he ah wan real anti-man.*

People think **that** he is a powerful man, but he is a weakling.

senseh-fowl /sˈɛnsɛ-fˈaʊl/

hen protective of eggs to be hatched

Example: *Me bin guh near ah **senseh-fowl** an e try bite meh.*

I went close to the **setting hen,** and she tried to peck me.

shap-clos /ʃap-kloz/

menstruation

Example: *De man seh plain-plain dat e wife tell am dat no sex tonight becaas **shap-close.***

The man said outrightly that his wife told him that there will be no intercourse tonight because she is **menstruating.**

she done get dig out /ʃɪ dʌn dɪg aʊt/

a woman who has had multiple partners

Example: *Uncle Tammy she dat nobady guh marrid dah gyaal becaas **she done get dig out.***

Uncle Tommy said that no-one would marry that girl since **she has already had multiple partners.**

shimmy /ʃˈɪmi/

clothing for babies

Example: *Me husband maamy buy waan cheap-cheap blue **shimmy** fuh we first baby girl.*

My husband's mother bought a cheap blue **top** for our first baby girl.

shine-eye /ʃˈɑɪn-ˈaɪ/

a hankering for material things

Example: *Uncle Fraser waan e son fuh keep way fram **shine-eye** gyaal.*

Uncle Fraser warned his son to avoid **greedy** girls.

shine-rice /ʃˈɑɪn-rˈaɪs/

dish of boiled rice, split peas and salted fish

Example:

Wen me daady laas he wuk, me mooma cook **shine-rice** *every day fuh wan mont straight.*

When my father lost his job, my mother cooked **shine rice** every day for a month.

shitabatee /ʃˈɪtˈɑbˈɑtˈiː/

a small boy

Example:

Dah lil **shitabattee** *bai does play big shat even do e nah get nuttin.*

That **stupid boy** is arrogant even though he is penniless.

shut-tail /ʃˈʌt-tˈeɪl/

small half-naked boy

Example:

De lawyer tell Harry dat he bin know am since e binna wan lil **shut-tail** *bai.*

The lawyer told Harry that he knew him since he was a **half-naked** boy.

side-dish /sɑɪd-dɪʃ/

lover of a married man or married woman

Example:

Nuff-nuff good-fuh-nuttin man an woman dese days get **side-dish.**

Lots of worthless men and women nowadays have **extra-marital affairs**.

side-kick /saɪd-kɪk/

best friend

Example: *Alan bin me **side-kick** since we lil, but now he rich, he does show-off.*

Alan was my **best friend** since youth, but now that he is rich, he shows off.

simetoo /sɪmʌtu:/

season seedy fruit, usually yellow in color

Example: *Me saarch ah whole maakit, but nobady get **simetoo** fuh sell.*

I searched the entire market, but no-one had **simetoo** to sell.

sirwah /sˈɪrwɑ/

gravy

Example: *Granny like she curry wid nuff-nuff **sirwah**.*

Granny likes her curry with lots of **gravy.**

skinnip /skˈɪnɪp/

genip

Example: *Dem seh dat if yuh eat **skinnip** seed, yuh guh get wapyah.*

They believe that eating **genip** seeds would give you blisters on your mouth.

skinora /skɪnoːrɑ/

eyes

Example: *Ah mango bin deh right front e **skinora** but e nah see am.*

The mango was right before his **eyes**, but he did not see it.

skulk /skʌlk/

to absent

Example: *Dah bai does **skulk** fram school three time a week.*

That boy **escapes** from school three days per week.

sky-juice /skɑɪ-dʒuːs/

rain

Example: *Wen me tell ah lady meh tusty, she tell meh fuh guh drink **sky-juice**.*

When I told the woman I was thirsty, she told me to go drink **rainwater**.

skylark /skˈɑɪlɑːrk/

idle

Example: *Nuff ah dem govament office worka does get pay fuh **skylark**.*

Many civil servants get paid to **idle**.

slash /slɑʃ/

to weed whack (a yard)

Example: *Alia fada does come evry three week fuh*
slash abee yaad.

Alia's father **weed whacks** our yard every
three-week period.

small-piece /smˈɑːl-pˈiːs/

money

Example: *Dese days yuh get parents who does send*
dem pickney fuh beg fuh small-piece.

Nowadays you have parents who send their
children to beg for **money.**

smokin hassar /smˈoːkɪn hˈɑsɑːr/

type of heavily shelled fish

Example: *Dem cane-cutta does ketch nuff-nuff*
smokin hassar in ah cane-piece.

Canecutters catch lots of **smoking hassar**
in the cane fields.

sometimeish /sˈʌmtaɪmɪʃ/

a moody person

Example: *Dah lady prapah **sometimeish**: one day,*
she nice-nice; nex day, she haggish.

That woman is terribly **moody**: one day,
she is very nice; the next day, she is rude.

son /sʌn/

swollen testicles

Example: *Dem pickney binna laugh Uncle Thomas*
son bad-bad.

The children laughed cruelly at Uncle
Thomas' **swollen testicles**.

souree /sˈaʊər͵iː/

finger-sized sour fruit

Example: *Nuff people does use souree fuh mek peppa*
sauce.

Lots of folks use the **belambee fruit** to
make pepper sauce.

spence /spˈɛns/

sperm

Example: *Me bin shack wen me see dah nice-nice*
hotel bedsheet stain wid spence.

I was shocked to see the bedsheets of the
expensive hotel stained with **sperm.**

spirit-gaan-pan-yuh /spɪrɪt-gɑːn-pɑn-yʊ/

to suddenly dislike

Example: *Me nah taak to dah bai fih wan day, an e*
staat complain dat meh spirit-gan-pan-he.

I did not speak to that boy for one day, and
he started to complain that I **suddenly**
disliked him.

spokan-ji /spˈoːkən-dʒˈi/

silly person

Example: *Me maamy bin seh dat me cousin is a real*
spokan-ji.

My mother said that my cousin was very
stupid.

spurwing /spˈʌrwɪŋ/

type of bird found at the sea-side

Example: *De bes rum-shap in Berbice does sell deep-*
fry spurwing, but yuh gat fuh aks fuh fine-
bud.

The best rum-shops in Berbice sell deep-
fried **spurwing** bird, which they call "fine
bird".

staan /stˈɑːn/

to stay

Example: *Ah pickney mooma warn am fuh staan*
right deh while she go in ah shap

The child's mother warned him **to remain**
where he was while she went into the shop.

staan /stˈɑːn/

to behave

Example: *Me nah know why dah gyaal staan suh.*

I have no idea why that girl **behaves** the
way she does.

staan-easy-beta-dan-beg-paaden /stɑ:-izi-bɛtɑ-dɑn-bɛg-pɑ:dn̩/

to remain silent than say something stupid

Example: *Me nani wary tell am dat **staan-easy-beta-dan-beg-paaden**.*

My grandmother always tells that girl to **keep quiet rather than say stupid things.**

staan-lil-bit /stˈɑ:n-lɪl-bɪt/

inviting a guest to stay a while

Example: *Me beg dem **fuh staan-lil-bit**, but dem just jump in dem cyaar an gaan.*

I asked them to **stay a while**, but they went into their car and drove away.

stable-bai /ste:bl̩-baɪ/

a lover of a married woman

Example: *Dah lady gat no shame how she deh all bout wid she schupit **stable-bai**.*

That woman is shameless in the way she goes everywhere with her stupid **lover.**

stave-aff /stev-ɑf/

to prevent

Example: *Abee put razah-wire pan abee fence fih **stave-aff** dem teef-man.*

We put razor-wire on our fence to prevent thieves from climbing over.

stchuups /ˌstˈʌːtsˈuːps/

sound made between teeth to show dissatisfaction or
disgust

Example: *Wen ah teecha tell ah gyaal fuh read she
book, de gyaal just* **stchuups** *she teet an
walk out de school.*

When the teacher told the girl to read her
book, the girl simply **sucked her teeth**
rudely and walked out of the school.

stinganettle /stˈɪɲɑnɛtəl/

fidgety person

Example: *Me neva see wan lil bai likka dah, likka he
get* **stinganettle** *in e rass.*

I never saw a little boy as **fidgety** as that,
as if he has ants in his pants.

strechah /strˈɛtʃə/

a type of elastic candy

Example: *Wen me binna primary school, dem lady
binna sell home-mek* **stretchah sweetee** *fuh
one cent.*

When I was in primary school, women
would sell home-made **sweets** for a single
cent.

suck-salt /sʌk-sɑlt/

to be without or to be penniless

Example: *E spen out all e money an now e ah* **suck-
salt.***

He spent out all of his money, and now he
is **penniless**.

suck-teeth /sˈʌk-tˈiːt/

sound made between teeth signifying disrespect, anger, dislike

Example:

Me aks dem big UG people weh abee get suck teeth fram, an dem look me likka me run aff meh head.

I asked those big University of Guyana lecturers where **suck teeth** originated, and they looked at me as if I were insane.

sue-sue /sˈʊː-sˈʊː/

to gossip

Example:

Nuff ah dem teecha does gada up an just sue-sue whole-whole day.

Many teachers just gather up and **gossip** all day.

sue-sue /sˈʊː-sˈʊː/

to urinate

Example:

Ah lil bai pull dunk e pants an sue-sue right weh me does eat.

The little boy pulled down his pants and **urinated** in my dining room.

sue-sue /sˈʊː-sˈʊː/

informal communal savings pool

Example:

Every mont abee does trow 5,000 dala sue-sue an collect am year-end.

Every month, we contribute 5,000 to a **savings pool** and collect the savings at the end of year.

suh /sˈʌ/

a particular characteristic of a person or direction

Example: *Dem tell dem police dat ah bai nah deh yah, he gaan **suh**.*

They told the police that the boy was not there, that he went **that way**.

sukanti /sˈʌːkɑːnti/

a supernatural being believed to possess children

Example: *During break-time, dem school chirrun does run bout like dem gat **sukanti**.*

During the break, the school children run around as if they were **possessed**.

sukanti /sˈʌːkɑːnti/

to feign illness

Example: *Whole day, me sista deh good-good, but wen anybady come, she do likka she get **sukanti**.*

My sister is well the entire day, but when anyone visits, she **feigns illness**.

suruh-and-duruh /sˈʌːrʌ-ˈɑn-dˈʌrʌ/

two close friends

Example: *Me tell am nah fuh get between dah husband an wife, dem two likka **suruh-and duruh**.*

I told him not to get in between that husband and wife, that they always get back **close**.

suskay /sˈʌskeɪ/

rapid intake of air after or during crying

Example: *Wen she lass she ambrella, she staat waan cry an **suskay** likka somebady beat she.*

When she lost her umbrella, she **wept** as if someone had beaten her.

swaar /sw ɑːr/

to fool

Example: *He try **swaar** ah big man fuh money, an e ketch two good slap fuh he pain.*

He tried to **con** the older man for money and got two good slaps for his effort.

swank /swɑnk/

a drink made of lime and sugar

Example: *Wen ah place hat-hat, me pickney dem does drink nuff-nuff **swank.***

When it is very hot, my children drink lots of **lime drink.**

sweet-man /swˈiːt -mɑn/

outside lover to a married woman

Example: *Dah lady nah get waan ounce shame how she deh hey an dey wid she blasted **sweet-man**.*

That woman has no shame whatsoever in the way she has her **lover** everywhere with her.

sweet-mout /swˈiːt-maʊt/

person who likes tasty foods

Example: *Devika get big an fat becaas she prapah get **sweet-mout**.*

Devika has got big and fat because she has a **sweet tooth.**

sweet-mout /swˈiːt-maʊt/

persuasive person

Example: *Dem sella in Port Mourant maakit get bad-bad **sweet-mout**.*

The vendors at Port Mourant market are good at **charming** people into buying.

sweet-woman /swˈiːt - ʌmɑn/

outside lover to a married man

Example: *Hussein binna wan rich-rich man, but e wase all e money pon nuf-nuf **sweet-woman**.*

Hussein was a very wealthy man, but he squandered all his money on **outside women.**

T t

tagga /tˈɑːɡə/

children's game

Example: *Chirrun dese days don even know de word **tagga** much less know how fuh play de game.*

Children nowadays do not even know the word much less know how to play **tagga**.

tailee /tɑɪliː/

a small pouch for money

Example: *Me nani does always put she **tailee** in she bosom.*

My grandmother always puts her **money pouch** in her bosom.

talk-man/tɑːk - mɑːn/

one who is good at giving speeches on any topic; person who talks incessantly

Example: *Dah politician is a real **talk-man,** but e don mek no sense to me.*

That politician can **talk a lot**, but he makes no sense.

tambran /tˈɑːmbrən/

tamarind

Example: *Me granpa does drink one glass **tambran** juice evry maanin.*

My grandpa drinks one glass of **tamarind** juice every morning.

tampolin /tˈɑmpoːlɪn/

tarpaulin

Example: *Abee had fuh put up nuff **tampolin** fuh me sista weddin in case rain come dung.*

We had to put up lots of **tarpaulin** for my sister's wedding in case of rain.

taw /tˈɔː/

children's game played with marbles

Example: ***Taw** binna wan nice-nice game abee binna play wid maable.*

Taw was a nice game that we played with marbles.

tawa /tˈɑːwə/

flat round metal pan for cooking

Example: *Me bin waan ah bai dat ah **tawa** hat-hat, but he haad-ayes an bun e haan.*

I warned the boy that the **flat disc used to cook** roti was hot, but he refused to listen and burned his hand.

tea /tˈiː/

generic name for all hot beverages

Example: *Aunty Lena aks ah man if e waan **tea** or coffee **tea** or milo **tea**.*

Aunty Lena asked the gentleman if he wanted **tea** or coffee or Milo.

tea /t'i:/

morning meal

Example: *Me daady like roti fuh e **tea** maanin time.*

My father likes roti for **breakfast**.

tek-foot /tɛk-fʊt/

begin to walk

Example: *Meh fren jump up wid shack an shout dat meh lil-lil puppy dem ah **tek-foot**.*

My friend jumped up and shouted excitedly that my little pups were **beginning to walk**.

tenney/ tɛni/

chamber pot

Example: *Me granny does still put she **tenney** undah she bed night-time.*

My granny still puts her **chamber-pot** under her bed at nights.

tick /t'ɪk/

heavy-legged female

Example: *Me fren Chotu seh he only like gyaal dat **tick**.*

My friend Chotu said that he likes only girls who are **heavy-legged**.

ticka /tˈɪkɑ/

black or red dot on forehead of females and babies

Example: *Uncle Ramchand seh dat all prapah Hindu gyaal must wear **ticka** pon dem forehead.*

Uncle Ramchand insisted that all proper Hindu females should wear a **dot** on their foreheads.

titivate /tˈɪtˈiːvˌeːt/

child or adult who likes to take apart or touch everything

Example: *Me ol man buy wan bran new car an staat **titivate** wid de engine right away.*

My father bought a brand- new car and immediately began to **experiment** with the engine.

tittah /tˈɪtˈɑː/

eldest sister

Example: *Me two **tittah** does prapah laugh how me does waak funny-funny.*

My two **elder sisters** really laugh at the way I walk.

towa-towa /tɑʊwɑ-tɑʊwɑ/

small singing bird

Example: *Me bin shack wen me hear how much dem bai does sell **towa-towa** fah.*

I was shocked to hear the price for a **towa-towa** bird.

truh-truh /trʊ-trʊ/

true

Example: *Wen e seh dat some story ah **truh-truh**, abee done know he done lie.*

When he claims that some story is **true**, we know that he is lying.

trup-chal /trʌp tʃˈɑɪl/

card game

Example: *Wen yuh guh wake house in Guyana, yuh betta prepare fuh play **trup-chal** whole night.*

When you go to a wake house in Guyana, you should prepare yourself to play the **trup-chal** card game for the entire night.

tuh-much-mout /tʊ-mʌtʃ-maʊt/

boastful

Example: *She get **tuh-much-mout** how ah tes easy-easy, but she fail am.*

She **boasted** how the test was simple, yet she failed it.

tuh-much-mout /tʊ-mʌtʃ-maʊt/

too many people to feed

Example: *Ah lady seh e gat fuh fine two-wuk becaas e get **tuh-much-mout** fuh feed.*

The woman said that she had to find two jobs because she had so **many children to feed.**

tunovah /tʌnovɑ/

a cake with red coconut filling

Example: *Sometimes we does call cocnut cake red-cake or salara, or **tunovah**.*

Sometimes we call coconut cake by the name of red-cake or salara or **tunovah.**

tutkah /tˈʊtkɑ/

belief involving actions

Example: *Wen me baby get hiccup, me mooma seh ah wan **tutkah** fuh put wan piece wet tread pan e forehead fuh ah hiccup done.*

When my baby has the hiccups, my mother said that it is a **belief** to place a piece of wet thread on the baby's forehead to stop the hiccup.

tutkah /tˈʊtkɑ/

ritual that ensures good fortune

Example: *You can do wan **tutkah** fuh bring good luck: just throw wan silva coin when yuh crass wata.*

You can do **a ritual** to ensure good fortune by throwing a silver coin into any body of water you cross.

twa-twa /twɔ-twɔ/

small singing bird

Example: *Wan **twa-twa** does sell fuh nuff money in Suriname.*

A **twa-twa** bird sells for a lot of money in Suriname.

V v

vagabone /vˈɑgɑbʌn/

thief; liar

Example: *Dah bai binna wan **vagabone** since he bin lil.*

That boy was a **vagabond** since he was a child.

W w

waday /wˈɑːdeɪ/

savory deep-fried dish of split peas and flour

Example: *Me mooma tell meh wife fuh mek nuff-nuff*
              ***waday** fuh abee baby nine-day.*

              My mother told my wife to make a great
              quantity of a **treat** she called waday for our
              baby's nine-day celebration.

wah-cum-sah-duh /wɑ-kʌm-sɑ-dʊ/

whatever will be will be

Example: *Me mooma does always seh dat **wah-cum-***
              sah duh.

              My mother always says **whatever will be
              will be.**

wan-wan /wɑn-wɑn/

little by little

Example: *Abee does always seh dat **wan-wan** dutty*
              buil damn.

              We always say that good things are built
              gradually.

wan-wan /wɑn-wɑn/

very few in number

Example: *Dah drunkee seh e does tek **wan-wan** shat fuh e birdday.*

That constantly drunk man claimed that he takes a **few** drinks of his birthday.

wapyah /wˈɑːpɪɑ/

whitening on sides of the mouth signaling vitamin deficiency

Example: *Granny tell we dat dah bai nah eat no fruit, so e done get **wapyah**.*

Grandma said that that boy does not eat fruits, so he has **scurvy**.

wara /wˈɑːrɑ/

small, thin-fleshed fruit, usually orange in color

Example: *Wen abee eat **wara**, abee teet does tun yella-yella.*

When we eat the **awara** fruit, our teeth become yellow.

wasteman /wˈeɪstmɑːn/

worthless person

Example: *Parmanan bin bright-bright wen abee bin in school, but now e wan real **wasteman**.*

Parmanand was very bright when we were in school, but now he is just **worthless**.

wata-cow /wɑtʌ-kɑʊ/

manatee

Example: *Wen we bin in school, dem had nuff **wata-cow** in de Botanical Gardens.*

     When I was in school, there were many **manatees** in the Botanical Gardens.

wata-nut /wˈɑːtˈɑː-nˈʌʊ/

lotus seed

Example: *Ah trench in front Berbice Campus full wid **wata-nut**.*

     The stream in front of the Berbice Campus is dense with **Lotus seeds.**

wata-soak /wˈɑːtˈɑː-sˈoːk/

soaked for a prolonged period in water

Example: *Me driva does run hide fan wan lil drizzle likka e brain guh get **wata-soak**.*

     My driver runs to hide from a mere drizzle as if it would **soak** his brain.

wata-wata /wˈɑːtˈɑ-wˈɑːtˈɑ/

tasteless

Example: *Devi mooma mek waan **wata-wata** curry.*

     Devi's mother made a **tasteless** curry.

wata-wata /wˈɑːtˈɑ-wˈɑːtˈɑ/

watery, soft

Example: *Yestaday me wife mek nice **wata-wata** all-in-wan.*

Yesterday my wife made a very good **watery** cook-up rice.

weddin-house /wɛdɪn-haʊs/

house where wedding is taking place

Example: *Me husband does always seh dat **weddin-house** food does taste bettah dan home food.*

My husband always says that **wedding-house** food tastes much better than home-cooked food.

wee-wee /wˈiː-wˈiː/

urine

Example: *Mr. London lil son bin too shame-face fuh **wee-wee** in de yard.*

Mr. London's small son was too shame-faced to **urinate** in the yard.

white-mout /wˈaɪt-mˈaʊt/

symptoms of scurvy or a deficiency of Vitamin C

Example: *Granny bin seh dat de bai get **white-mout** becaas he nah eat no fruits.*

Granny said that **the side of his lips are whitened** because he eats no fruit.

white-mout /wˈaɪt-mˈaʊt/

hungry

Example: *Me son fren dem does come hey an eat out all meh food likka dem all **white-mout.***

My son's friends always come home here and gobble up my food as if they were all **starving.**

wickedness /wɪkɪdnɪs/

a child's term for sexual intercourse

Example: *Ah lil gyaal threaten she big buddy dat she guh tell dem parents how she see he an e gyaal-fren binna do **wickedness.***

The little girl threatened her big brother that she will tell their parents about seeing them having **intercourse.**

wife-man /wˈaɪf-mˈɑn/

one who frequently seeks new sexual encounters

Example: *Uncle Soodial binna wan real **wife-man** wen e bin young.*

Uncle Soodial was a real **philanderer** when he was young.

willie /wˈɪli/

penis

Example: *Dah wutless lil bai does tek out he lil willie an show dem lil gyaal.*

That naughty little boy takes out his little penis and shows the little girls.

wiri-wiri /wˈɪri-wˈɪri/

small round pepper

Example: *Me does put five or six **wiri-wiri** in meh all-in-waan.*

I usually put five or six **small round peppers** when I make cook-up rice.

wisi-wisi duck /wˈɪsi-wˈɪsi dˈʌk/

type of duck, usually brown or dark blue

Example: *Mos people in Essequibo like **wisi-wisi duck** ovah white duck.*

Most people in Essequibo prefer **wisi-wisi duck** over white duck.

woman-rain /wˈʊmɑn-rˈeːn/

a constant drizzle

Example: *Dem had to stap de cricket match becaas ah **woman-rain.***

They had to stop the cricket match because of the **constant drizzle.**

wuk /wˈʌk/

commemorative event

Example: *Evry year dem does do wan **wuk** for dem mooma.*

Every year they have a commemorative ceremony for their deceased mother.

wukaholic /wˌʌːkɑhˈɑːlɪk/

someone who is constantly working, workaholic

Example: *Me tell dah **wukaholic** man dat e kyaan
done wuk, but wuk can done he.*

I told that **workaholic** that he cannot finish
work, but work can end his life.

wutless /wˈʌtlɪs/

worthless

Example: *Dah jail-bird bin **wutless** since he binna
guh primary school.*

That jail-bird was **worthless** since he was
in primary school.

Y y

yallah /jˈælɑ/

ripened

Example: *Abee does put green mangro in rice bag fuh e tun **yallah**.*

We used to put green mangoes in a rice bag so that it **ripens.**

yallah-batee /jˈælɑ-bˈatˈiː/

fair-skinned person

Example: *Abee use to tease ah man bout e **yallah-battie**, but now abee ah beg dah man fuh wan lil jaab.*

We used to tease that fair-skinned man about his **yellow backside**, but now we are all begging him for employment.

yasuh /jɑsʌ/

to be here

Example: *Dem does only come **yasuh** wen dem hungry fuh dead.*

They only **come here** when they are almost starved to death.

yawaree /jˈɑwɑriː/

large rodent famous for stealing fruits

Example: *Dem get two **yawaree** dat does teef all dem fruits pon abee fruit tree.*

There are two **rodents** who steal all the fruits from our fruit trees.

yawzee /jˈɑːziː/

sores, skin disease

Example: *Dah lady does wear shaat-shaat dress likka she waan show aff she **yawzee** foot dem.*

That woman wears very short dresses as if she wants to advertise the many **sores** on her legs.

youthman /jˈuːtmɑːn/

any young fellow

Example: *Nuff **youthman** dese days is just smokey.*

Many **male youths** these days are drug users.

yuh /jˈʌ/

you

Example: ***Yuh** bin waan me bout dah gyaal, but me nah listen.*

You had warned me against that girl, but I failed to take heed.

yuh-cry-pon-meh /jʊ-krɑɪ-pʌn-mɪ/

to give bad luck

Example: *No matta how haad meh wuk, meh wife **cry-pon-me** suh much dat meh kyaan see meh way.*

No matter how hard I work, my wife **complains** so much that I cannot seem to get ahead.

yuh do good, yuh hol wood /yʊ dʌ gʊd, yʊ ho:l wʌd/

unappreciated kindness

Example: *Uncle Denny swear dat wen **yuh do good, yuh hol wood**.*

Uncle Denny insists that when **you do good deeds you are left empty-handed.**

yuh know how e deh /jʌ-no-hɑʊ-i-dɛ/

you know his/her ways/attitudes/moods

Example: *He wife does ignore she husband nasty behaviah an seh **"yuh know how e deh"**.*

His wife excuses his bad behavior by saying **"you know how he is"**.